# WORKING —
# TEN-FRAMES

## Activities for Counting • Operations and Algebraic Thinking • Base Ten

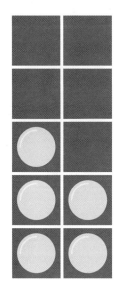

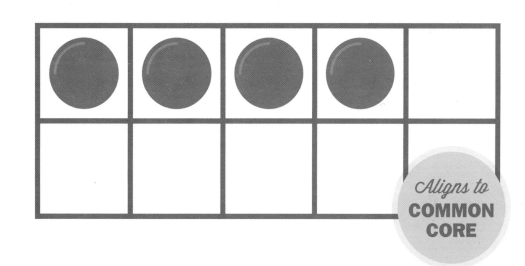

*Aligns to* **COMMON CORE**

BY
**DON S. BALKA**
AND
**RUTH HARBIN MILES**

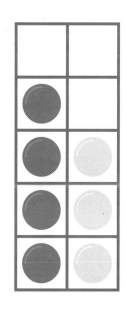

Order Number 211496
ISBN 978-1-58324-657-3

C D E F G 19 18 17 16 15

395 Main Street
Rowley, MA 01969
www.didax.com

# Table of Contents

# Introduction

Ten-frames are one of the most useful tools available to teachers for mathematics instruction and learning in the primary grades. Regardless of what type of markers, stickers, or color of crayons are used to fill, shade, or empty ten-frames, the model provides a visual presentation of mathematics that gives young children a firm base for starting their ventures with the content.

In this book, we offer a multitude of games and activities using ten-frames. They are all referenced to the Common Core State Standards for Mathematics and the related Standards for Mathematical Practice. Teachers from non-adopting states will have no difficulty finding appropriate activities for early number ideas.

Using ten-frames is not a new idea for teaching numeracy. Many books and articles have been written, and a multitude of different types of frames have been produced. Didax offers a variety of materials, from plastic ten-frame trains to giant magnetic ten-frames to foam ten-frames. Now, with technology at the forefront, online activities with ten-frames are also readily available.

From our classroom experiences, we have written and assembled this collection to focus on the main Common Core numeracy areas of Grades K–1: Counting and Cardinality, Operations and Algebraic Thinking, and Number and Operations in Base Ten. These three domains form the foundation for mathematics learning in higher grades.

A ten-frame is a 2 × 5 rectangular array of squares. The size of the squares is not a critical factor in using the frames. Ten-frames use the concept of two benchmark numbers, 5 and 10, to help students develop visual images for each number. Mathematics educators have observed students using ten-frames for many years. Those observations have led to many important recommendations for teachers to consider as they use ten-frames, none more important than the idea of subitization.

## Subitizing

Subitizing is the ability to perceive at a glance the number of items presented in a group without counting. This apparent innate ability allows students to make sudden mental images of certain arrangements of dots or other objects and then write the number or reproduce a representation of the quantity. The best example of subitization for adults to understand is the pattern of dots on regular six-sided dice or dominoes.

At a glance, we know there are five dots on the "X" pattern face; we do not need to count one by one to determine the "fiveness" of the face. Even double dominoes, with dot patterns up to 12, provide opportunities for subitization; however, we are generally more comfortable in our subitizing with lesser quantities.

Using ten-frames provides another avenue for subitization. Students observe one complete row of a frame shaded or covered; they "know" the frame represents five without counting individual cells. Similarly, they "see" six as one more than five, or double three, or an even number.

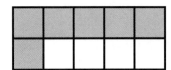

Seven is one more than 6, or 4 plus 3, . . .

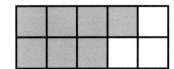

or one less than 8, or 3 less than 10, and an odd number.

As we have described, subitizing with a single ten-frame strengthens initial work with counting to higher numbers and with addition and subtraction. This understanding of numeracy or quantity does provide a needed basis for the mathematics learning that follows.

## Counting

Counting is the main way young children learn to construct number relationships. Prior to kindergarten, many children are taught to count orally. At the early primary level, students learn to count objects in a set, compare sets or numerals, and model joining and separating sets of objects. At this age, young children learn to draw pictures or write simple equations such as $4 + 2 = 6$ and $6 - 2 = 4$. The activities in this book will help children attach meaning to counting, which is critical to developing all number concepts. The focus on ten-frame activities will actively engage young students in making sense of counting and will help them be able to compose and decompose numbers in operations.

## Composition and Decomposition

Composing and decomposing numbers focuses on number pairs and is a fundamental component of number sense. Primary-grade students should use objects such as Unifix Cubes, two-color counters, square tiles, or other types of markers to compose or decompose different number pairs for a given number. For example, the number 10 may be composed (made up) or decomposed (broken down) into a set of 9 objects and 1, 8 objects and 2, 7 objects and 3, and so on. Ten-frames used with Unifix Cubes or two-color counters help kindergarten and first-grade students learn to visualize the relationships, groupings, and patterns in numbers. An understanding of how the number 10 is composed and decomposed is a prerequisite skill for place value understanding and quick mental calculations.

## Place Value

To understand place value, young children need to be able to make groups of 10 items and count the groups as a single item—for example, 14 means one group of ten and four ones. Children also need to understand that the digits can have different values depending on the "place" or position of the number. Each place has a value of 10 times the place to its right. Young children may be able to read a two-digit numbers such as 34 or 43 but may not understand what each number represents or why the numbers have different values. The use of ten-frames supports the developmental foundation for place value understanding. To help students comprehend place value, two ten-frames placed side by side (left to right) may be used.

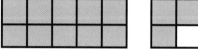 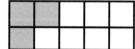

The first ten-frame represents a quantity of 10 units or one group of 10. The second frame represents individual ones.

The two side-by-side frames provide a visual to help students make sense of place value.

## Summary

The games and activities in this book incorporate ten-frames to support students in visualizing, modeling, and internalizing abstract concepts. The ten-frames tools help students attach meaning to counting, build number sense, learn to subitize, compare whole numbers, gain quick mental calculation skills, compose and decompose numbers, and develop an understanding of place value. They also support the development of addition and subtraction. The activities will actively engage your students and help promote achievement in mathematics.

— Don S. Balka and Ruth Harbin Miles

# Correlation to Common Core State Standards

| Standard[1,2] | Activity No. |
|---|---|
| **Grade K** | |
| **Counting and Cardinality (K.CC)** | |
| Know number names and the count sequence. (K.CC.1–3) | 1, 2, 3, 4, 7, 11, 12 |
| Count to tell the number of objects. (K.CC.4–5) | 1, 2, 5, 6, 7, 8, 9, 19 |
| Compare numbers. (K.CC.6–7) | 10, 11, 12, 40 |
| **Operations and Algebraic Thinking (K.OA)** | |
| Understand addition as putting together and adding to, and undersand subtraction as taking apart and taking from. (K.OA.1–5) | 6, 13, 14, 15, 16, 17, 18, 19, 20, 21 |
| **Number and Operations in Base Ten (K.NBT)** | |
| Work with numbers 11–19 to gain foundations for place value. (K.NBT.1) | 22, 23, 24, 25 |
| **Grade 1** | |
| **Operations and Algebraic Thinking (1.OA)** | |
| Represent and solve problems involving addition and subtraction. (1.OA.1–2) | 26, 27, 28, 29, 30, 31 |
| Understand and apply properties of operations and the relationship between addition and subtraction. (1.OA.3–4) | 32, 33, 34 |
| Add and subtract within 20. (1.OA.5–6) | 30, 32, 33, 34, 35, 36, 37, 38, 39, 40, 41, 42, 43, 47, 49, 50 |
| **Number and Operations in Base Ten (1.NBT)** | |
| Understand place value. (1.NBT.2–3) | 2, 11, 12, 28, 43, 44 |
| Use place value understanding and properties of operations to add and subtract. (1.NBT.4–6) | 45, 46, 47, 48, 49 |

[1] Standards not correlated to the activities in this book are not listed.

[2] See teacher pages for a more detailed correlation of each activity to the standard listed.

# Working with Ten-Frames

# 1: Make a Match

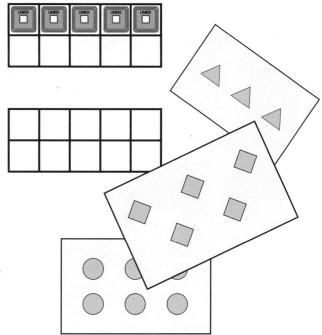

## ⓘ Number of Students

Individual, small group, or entire class

## ⊘ Materials

For each student:
- 1 or 2 ten-frames or Ten-Frames Template (page 110)
- 10 or 20 Unifix Cubes or other markers

For each group:
- Object Cards (pages 111–113)

## ◈ Overview

In this activity, students place Unifix Cubes or other markers in one or two ten-frames corresponding to the number of objects shown on the Object Cards.

## Common Core State Standards

### Content Standards:

**Grade Level:** K

**Domain:** Counting and Cardinality (K.CC)

**Know number names and the count sequence.**

1. Count to 100 by ones and tens.

**Count to tell the number of objects.**

4. Understand the relationship between numbers and quantities; connect counting to cardinality.

   a. When counting objects, say the number names in the standard order, pairing each object with one and only one number name and each number name with one and only one object.

   b. Understand that the last number name said tells the number of objects counted. The number of objects is the same regardless of their arrangement or the order in which they were counted.

5. Count to answer "how many?" questions about as many as 20 things arranged in a line, a rectangular array, or a circle, or as many as 10 things in a scattered configuration; given a number from 1–20, count out that many objects.

### Practice Standards:

1. **Make sense of problems and persevere in solving them.**

   Kindergarten students are beginning their mathematics learning. They are focusing on one-to-one correspondence by matching Unifix Cubes to the objects on cards or using their fingers to count the objects and then placing Unifix Cubes on the ten-frame(s).

2. **Reason abstractly and quantitatively.**

   Students must be able to "transfer" a quantity represented on the Object Cards to the ten-frame(s), and then state the corresponding number.

# ⬛ Presenting the Activity

1. Make copies of the Object Cards and cut them apart.

2. Distribute up to 20 Unifix Cubes of any color or other appropriate markers to each student.

3. Say to the student(s):

   ❝ Here is a card with some shapes on it.

   Place your Unifix Cubes on the ten-frame(s) to show me the same number of cubes as there are shapes.

   Then tell me how many cubes there are.

4. You may need to demonstrate the activity with one card.

5. Allow time for students to complete the task.

6. Say to the student(s):

   ❝ Now, here is another card with shapes.

   Show me the same number of Unifix Cubes as there are (triangles, circles, and so on).

7. Repeat the activity for at least five Object Cards.

# ⊘ Assessing Student Responses

The following questions will help you assess your students' responses to the activity:

• Did the student(s) match the cubes correctly for each card?

• Did the student(s) state the correct number of cubes for each card?

• What procedure did the student(s) use to make the matches? Did they count the objects first and then count the corresponding number of cubes? Did they place a Unifix Cube on top of or next to each object on the Object Card, and then transfer the cubes to the ten-frame(s)?

• Did the student(s) have difficulty with higher numbers? Did they have to recount for certain matches?

# 2: Concentration

## (i) Number of Students

Partner pairs or small group

## (/) Materials

For each group:
- Ten-Frame Cards 1–20 (pages 114–116)
- Number Cards 1–20 (pages 117–119)
- Colored paper

## (◈) Overview

In this activity, students match Ten-Frame Cards to corresponding Number Cards.

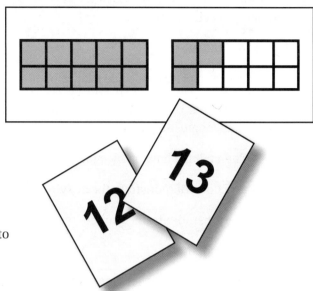

## Common Core State Standards

### Content Standards:

**Grade Level:** K

**Domain:** Counting and Cardinality (K.CC)

**Know number names and the count sequence.**

1. Count to 100 by ones and tens.

**Count to tell the number of objects.**

4. Understand the relationship between numbers and quantities; connect counting to cardinality.

   a. When counting objects, say the number names in the standard order, pairing each object with one and only one number name and each number name with one and only one object.

   b. Understand that the last number name said tells the number of objects counted. The number of objects is the same regardless of their arrangement or the order in which they were counted.

5. Count to answer "how many?" questions about as many as 20 things arranged in a line, a rectangular array, or a circle, or as many as 10 things in a scattered configuration; given a number from 1–20, count out that many objects.

**Grade Level:** 1

**Domain:** Number and Operations in Base Ten (1.NBT)

**Understand place value.**

2. Understand that the two digits of a two-digit number represent amounts of tens and ones. Understand the following as special cases:

   a. 10 can be thought of as a bundle of ten ones — called a "ten."

   b. The numbers from 11 to 19 are composed of a ten and one, two, three, four, five, six, seven, eight, or nine ones.

### Practice Standards:

2. **Reason abstractly and quantitatively.**

   Kindergarten students must be able to "transfer" a quantity represented on the Ten-Frame Cards to the corresponding number card. In Grade 1, the thinking continues with numbers up to 20, with a focus on tens.

7. **Look for and make use of structure.**

   Grade 1 students are beginning their study of place value. They are focusing on numbers 11–19. Two ten-frames are necessary, with one always completely filled.

## ⊡ Presenting Activity 1

1. Make copies of the Ten-Frame Cards and Number Cards using different-colored paper for the two sets of cards. Cut them apart.

2. Distribute both sets of cards to each group of students.

3. Say to the student(s):

   > 🔊 Place all of the Ten-Frame Cards faceup in two rows.
   >
   > Place all of the Number Cards faceup in two rows.

4. You may need to demonstrate how to place the two sets of cards.

5. Allow time for students to complete the task.

6. Say to the students:

   > 🔊 Now, one of you starts by matching one Ten-Frame Card with the corresponding Number Card. Pick up the two cards and place them in a pile.
   >
   > Take turns making matches until you have matched all the cards.

## ⊡ Presenting Activity 2

1. Make copies of the Ten-Frame Cards and Number Cards using different-colored paper for the two sets of cards. Cut them apart.

2. Distribute both sets of cards to each group of students.

3. Say to the students:

   > 🔊 Place all of the Ten-Frame Cards facedown in two rows.
   >
   > Place all of the Number Cards facedown in two rows.

4. You may need to demonstrate how to place the two sets of cards.

5. Allow time for students to complete the task.

6. Say to the students:

   > 🔊 Now, one of you starts by turning one Ten-Frame Card and one Number Card. If the two cards match, pick them up and place them in a pile. If they do not match, turn them over.
   >
   > Take turns making matches until you have matched all the cards.

## ⊘ Assessing Student Responses

The following questions will help you assess your students' responses to the activity:

- Did the student(s) match the Ten-Frame Cards and Number Cards correctly?

- Did numbers in the teens cause difficulty for students? What did you observe?

- What procedure did the student(s) use to make the matches? Did they count the objects on the ten-frames first and then find the corresponding number? Did they notice that one frame was completely filled and just count the markers on the second ten-frame?

# 3: I've Got Your Number

## ⓘ Number of Students

Partner pairs or entire class

## ⊘ Materials

For each student:

- 10 blank Cell Phone Picture Cards (page 116)
- Pencil

For the teacher:

- Ten-Frames Template (page 110)
- 20 Unifix Cubes
- Document camera projection device

## ◉ Overview

In this activity, the teacher will use a document camera to project Unifix Cubes on a ten-frame. Students will count the number of cubes and write the number they see.

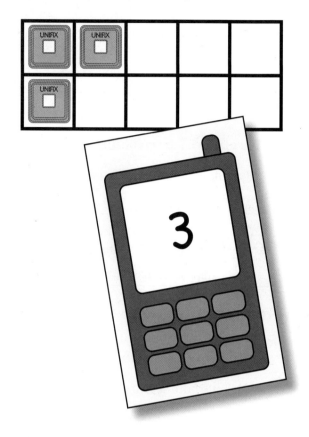

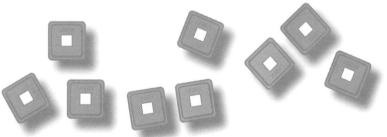

## Common Core State Standards

**Content Standards:**

**Grade Level:** K

**Domain:** Counting and Cardinality (K.CC)

**Know number names and the count sequence.**

3. Write numbers from 0 to 20. Represent a number of objects with a written numeral 0–20 (with 0 representing a count of no objects).

**Practice Standards:**

2. **Reason abstractly and quantitatively.**

Students must make sense of the quantity involved in each number called.

# ⊡ Presenting the Activity

1. Reproduce 10 blank Cell Phone Picture Cards for each student.

2. Distribute a pencil to each student.

3. Say to the students:

   **( " )** I will show you a ten-frame with Unifix Cubes. Count the number of cubes you see.

   Write that number of cubes on one of your cell phone cards.

   Here is an example. How many cubes do you see?

   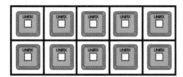

4. Say to the students:

   **( " )** You will use your pencil to write 20 on the first cell phone card.

5. As a quick "every pupil response," have students hold up their cell phone cards to show 20.

6. Continue using the ten-frames and Unifix Cubes with students to count and write the numbers they see.

# ⊙ Assessing Student Responses

The following questions will help you assess your students' responses to the activity.

- Did the student(s) correctly count the number of objects shown?

- Did the student(s) correctly write the number?

- Could the student(s) count the number, but not write the number?

- Did the student(s) reverse the two digits of the written numbers? (For example, did a student write "41" for the called number "14"? Number reversals are a developmental issue for kindergarten students that should be pointed out by modeling the correct number.

- Did the student(s) think of the teen numbers as a group of one ten and more ones?

# 4: Count and Write My Number

## ⓘ Number of Students

Partner pairs or entire class

## ⊘ Materials

For each pair of students:
- 2 Ten-Frames Templates (page 110)
- 20 Unifix Cubes
- Six-sided number cube (1–6)

For each student:
- Individual whiteboard and marker (or create a recording sheet)

For the teacher:
- Number Cards 0–20 (pages 117–119)
- Document camera, if available

## ◈ Overview

In this activity, students will use Unifix Cubes and ten-frames to count and demonstrate the numbers called. Students will write the numbers on individual student whiteboards.

---

## Common Core State Standards

**Content Standards:**

**Grade Level:** K

**Domain:** Counting and Cardinality (K.CC)

**Know number names and the count sequence.**

3. Write numbers from 0 to 20. Represent a number of objects with a written numeral 0–20 (with 0 representing a count of no objects).

**Practice Standards:**

2. **Reason abstractly and quantitatively.**

   Students must make sense of the quantity involved in each number called.

7. **Look for and make use of structure.**

   Students must learn to subitize, recognizing the number 14 is one ten and four ones.

---

# ◉ Presenting the Activity

1. Reproduce the Number Cards 0–20 and cut the cards apart. Have each partner pair shuffle the cards and place them facedown.

2. Reproduce and distribute 2 Ten-Frames Templates to the partner pairs.

3. Distribute 20 Unifix Cubes to each partner pair.

4. Distribute individual student whiteboards and markers to each student.

5. Have students roll the number cube. The player who rolls the greater number will be Player 1.

6. Say to the students:

   " I will call a number. Player 1 will use the Unifix Cubes and ten-frames to show the number called. For example, if I call the number 3, Player 1 will count out three Unifix Cubes and place them on the frame like this:

7. Say to the students:

   " Player 2 will check Player 1's work. If correct, Player 2 will write the number on the whiteboard.

   Player 1 will check to see whether the written number is correct.

   I will show you the number called using the card and our document camera.

8. Call another number and repeat the activity. This time have Player 2 count out the cubes to be placed on the ten-frames. Have Player 1 check for correctness and then write the number on the recording sheet or whiteboard.

9. Continue with several more numbers as time allows.

# ◉ Assessing Student Responses

The following questions will help you assess your students' responses to the activity.

- Did the student(s) correctly count and demonstrate the numbers called?

- Did the student(s) correctly write the numbers?

- Could the student(s) count the numbers, but not write the numbers?

- Did the student(s) reverse the digits of the two-digit numbers? (For example, did a student write "31" for the called number "13"? Number reversals are a developmental issue for kindergarten students and should be pointed out by modeling the correct number.

- Did the student(s) use one-to-one correspondence when placing and counting the Unifix Cubes on the ten-frames?

- Did the student(s) think of the teen numbers as a group of one ten and more ones?

# 5: Number Words

## ⓘ Number of Students

Individual or partner pairs

## ⊘ Materials

For each student or pair of students:

- 2 ten-frames or Ten-Frames Template (page 110)
- Number Word Cards "one" to "twenty" (page 121–122)
- 20 Unifix Cubes (two colors)
- Paper bag

## ◈ Overview

There are two activities for "Number Words." In Activity 1, students place Unifix Cubes or other markers corresponding to number words "one" through "twenty" on one or two ten-frames.

In Activity 2, students grab Unifix Cubes from a bag, place them on the ten-frames, and then find the Number Word Card that corresponds to the number of cubes.

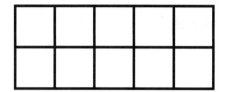

## Common Core State Standards

### Content Standards:

**Grade Level:** K

**Domain:** Counting and Cardinality (K.CC)

**Count to tell the number of objects.**

5. Count to answer "how many?" questions about as many as 20 things arranged in a line, a rectangular array, or a circle, or as many as 10 things in a scattered configuration; given a number from 1–20, count out that many objects.

### Practice Standards:

4. **Model with mathematics.**

   Students use manipulatives to model a specified number.

7. **Look for and make use of structure.**

   As students continue modeling numbers 1–20 on the ten-frames, they begin to notice patterns in the arrangement of Unifix Cubes. The representations in the ten-frames help them as they begin addition activities.

# 📑 Presenting Activity 1

1. Make copies of the Number Word Cards on card stock and cut them apart.

2. Distribute 20 Unifix Cubes or other markers to each student.

3. Say to the student(s):

   > 66 Draw a Number Word Card and fill the ten-frames with the corresponding number of Unifix Cubes.

4. You may need to demonstrate the activity with one card.

5. Allow time for students to complete the task.

6. Say to the student(s):

   > 66 Now, how many more Unifix Cubes do you need to make 10 (20)? Use the other color of Unifix Cubes to fill in the ten-frame.

7. Repeat the activity for at least 10 Number Word Cards.

8. For each Number Word Card drawn, say to student(s):

   > 66 Write your number on paper. For example, if you draw "ten," write "10."

# 📑 Presenting Activity 2

1. Make copies of the Number Word Cards on card stock and cut them apart.

2. Distribute a paper bag containing 20 Unifix Cubes or other markers and 2 ten-frames or the Ten-Frames Template to each student or pair.

3. Say to the student(s):

   > 66 Grab a handful of Unifix Cubes from the bag and place them on your ten-frames. Then find the Number Word Card that corresponds to the number of cubes on the ten-frames. For example, if you have 12 cubes on your frames, find the Number Word Card that says "twelve."

4. You may need to demonstrate the activity with one card.

5. Allow time for students to complete the task.

6. Say to the student(s):

   > 66 When you're finished with one grab from the paper bag, place the Unifix Cubes back in the bag and grab another handful of cubes.

7. Repeat the activity for at least 10 Number Word Cards.

# ◉ Assessing Student Responses

The following questions will help you assess your students' responses to the activities:

- Did the student(s) show the correct number of cubes for each Number Word Card?

- If the student(s) showed an incorrect number of Unifix Cubes, what error did they make? Did they skip numbers as they counted? Did they have difficulty reading the number word? Did they have difficulty with any number in the teens?

- Did the student(s) use any special procedures in counting the cubes? Did they make a pile of cubes before placing them on the ten-frames?

- For Activity 2, did the student(s) find the corresponding Number Word Card for each grab from the bag?

# 6: One More Than/One Less Than

## ⓘ Number of Students

Individuals or pairs

## ⊘ Materials

For each student:

- 2 ten-frames or Ten-Frames Template (page 110)
- "One More Than/One Less Than" Recording Sheets (pages 123–124)
- 13 Unifix Cubes of one color or other markers

For each pair of students:

- Number Cards 1–13 (pages 117–118)

## ◈ Overview

In this activity, students place Unifix Cubes in a ten-frame to show one more or one less than a specific number of cubes.

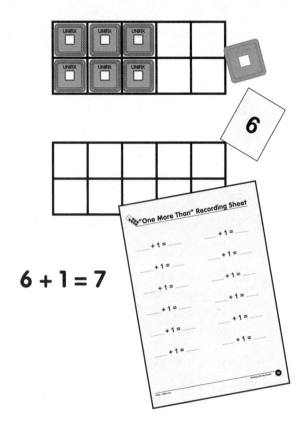

$$6 + 1 = 7$$

## Common Core State Standards

### Content Standards:

**Grade Level:** K

**Domain:** Counting and Cardinality (K.CC)

**Count to tell the number of objects.**

4. Understand the relationship between numbers and quantities; connect counting to cardinality.

   c. Understand that each successive number name refers to a quantity that is one larger.

**Domain:** Operations and Algebraic Thinking (K.OA)

**Understand addition as putting together and adding to, and understand subtraction as taking apart and taking from.**

2. Solve addition and subtraction word problems, and add or subtract within 10, e.g., by using objects or drawings to represent the problem.

### Practice Standards:

1. **Model with mathematics.**

   Students are using manipulatives to model basic addition and subtraction facts within 10. From the visual representations they create with their ten-frames, they are stating or writing the corresponding addition or subtraction equation on a recording sheet. For example, $3 + 1 = 4$ or $8 - 1 = 7$.

7. **Look for and make use of structure.**

   Kindergarten students learn that any whole number is one more than the preceding number, and that any whole number is one less than the next consecutive whole number.

# ◉ Presenting the Activity

1. Make copies of the Number Cards on card stock and cut them apart.

2. Distribute 2 ten-frames or the Ten-Frames Template, 13 Unifix Cubes of one color or other markers, and a recording sheet to each student.

3. Distribute a set of Number Cards to each pair.

4. Say to the student(s):

   Place the Number Cards facedown in front of you.

5. Say to the student(s):

   **(66)** Now, draw a Number Card from the pile. Use your Unifix Cubes to show one more than the number on your card.

6. Repeat the activity for all 13 Number Cards. For each Number Card drawn, say to the student(s):

   **(66)** On your recording sheet, write the number from the card in the first space, and then write the total number of cubes in the second space: $3 + 1 = 4$.

7. Allow time for students to complete the task.

8. Say to the student(s):

   **(66)** Now, reshuffle the cards and place them facedown in front of you. Draw a card from the pile. Use your Unifix Cubes to show one less than the number on your card.

9. Repeat the activity for all 13 Number Cards. For each Number Card drawn, say to student(s):

   **(66)** On your recording sheet, write the number from the card in the first space, and then write the total number of cubes in the second space: $\underline{6} - 1 = \underline{5}$.

10. Allow time for the students to complete the task.

# ◉ Assessing Student Responses

The following questions will help you assess students' responses to the activity:

- Did the student(s) correctly show the number of cubes corresponding to *one more than* or *one less than* the number shown on the card?

- Did the student(s) have difficulty with any particular number?

- What procedure did the student(s) use to show *one more than* or *one less than*? Did the student count out the number of cubes shown on the card and then add (subtract) one, or did the student count out directly the appropriate number of cubes and place them in the frame?

# 7: Find It on the Floor

## ⓘ Number of Students

Small group or entire class

## ⊘ Materials

- Ten-Frame Cards 1–20 (pages 114–115)
- Teacher-created number cards (1–10 or 1–20) on 8.5 × 11 in. paper

## ◈ Overview

In this activity, students match representations of numbers on ten-frames to corresponding numbers placed on the floor.

## Common Core State Standards

### Content Standards:

**Grade Level:** K

**Domain:** Counting and Cardinality (K.CC)

**Know number names and the count sequence.**

1. Count to 100 by ones and tens.

**Count to tell the number of objects.**

4. Understand the relationship between numbers and quantities; connect counting to cardinality.

   a. When counting objects, say the number names in the standard order, pairing each object with one and only one number name and each number name with one and only one object.

   b. Understand that the last number name said tells the number of objects counted. The number of objects is the same regardless of their arrangement or the order in which they were counted.

5. Count to answer "how many?" questions about as many as 20 things arranged in a line, a rectangular array, or a circle, or as many as 10 things in a scattered configuration; given a number from 1–20, count out that many objects.

### Practice Standards:

1. **Make sense of problems and persevere in solving them.**

   Kindergarten students are beginning their mathematics learning. They are matching the representation of a quantity on a ten-frame with the corresponding numeral.

2. **Reason abstractly and quantitatively.**

   Students must be able to "transfer" a quantity represented on the ten-frames to the corresponding number.

# Presenting the Activity

1. Make copies of the Ten-Frame Cards (1–10 or 1–20) and distribute one card to each student.

2. Write the numbers 1 to 10, or 1 to 20, on separate sheets of 8.5 × 11 in. paper.

3. Randomly place these informal number cards on the floor.

4. Say to the students:

   > When I say "Go!" I want you to find the number on the floor that matches the number represented on your ten-frame.
   >
   > When you find it, come to the front of the room and line up in order from 1 to 10 (or 1 to 20).

5. You may need to demonstrate the activity with one ten-frame and one number card.

6. Allow time for students to complete the activity.

7. Say to the students:

   > When we finish, I will mix up the ten-frames and we will try again.

8. Repeat the activity at least three times.

# Assessing Student Responses

The following questions will help you assess your students' responses to the activity:

- Did the student(s) match the ten-frame correctly to the corresponding number card?

- Did the student(s) order the numbers correctly? If not, were certain numbers problematic?

- What procedure did the student(s) use to make the matches? Did they count the objects on their ten-frame one by one? Did they know what the corresponding number was just by looking?

- Did the student(s) have difficulty with higher numbers? Did they have to recount on the ten-frame to make certain matches?

# 8: Stand Up and Be Counted

## ⓘ Number of Students

Entire class

## ⊘ Materials

- 2 ten-frames or Ten-Frames Template (page 110)
- Number Cards 6–20 (pages 117–119)
- 20 Unifix Cubes
- Document camera or projection device

## ◈ Overview

In this teacher-directed activity, students will practice counting strategies with up to 20 objects.

## Common Core State Standards

### Content Standards:

**Grade Level:** K

**Domain:** Counting and Cardinality (K.CC)

**Count to tell the number of objects.**

5. Count to answer "how many?" questions about as many as 20 things arranged in a line, a rectangular array, or a circle, or as many as 10 things in a scattered configuration; given a number from 1–20, count out that many objects.

### Practice Standards:

2. **Reason abstractly and quantitatively.**

Students must make sense of the quantity in each grouping of cubes.

# (📖) Presenting the Activity

1. Distribute one number card to each student.

2. Say to the students:

   (❝) I will show you some Unifix Cubes. Count the cubes.

   I will say, "Stand up and be counted." If you have the card with the number that matches the cubes, you will stand up and hold up your card.

   You will explain to us how you grouped your cubes for counting, and then you will count the cubes for your classmates.

3. Continue with the activity by displaying several Unifix Cube groupings for students to count, like the examples shown at right.

4. If the objects you show are in a circle, the students must decide a starting point to begin the count.

5. If the objects you show are scattered, the students could explain how they regrouped the cubes, or perhaps how they found a pattern in the cube arrangement.

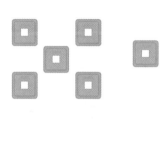

# (◉) Assessing Student Responses

The following questions will help you assess your students' responses to the activity.

- Did the student(s) use one-to-one correspondence to count correctly?

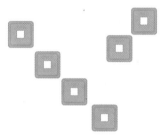

- Did the student(s) explain the grouping strategy they used?

- Did the student(s) move the objects into a pattern?

- Did the student(s) explain where they started counting in a scattered configuration?

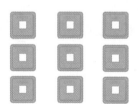

# 9: Flashing Numbers

## ⓘ Number of Students

Entire class

## ⊘ Materials

- For each student:
- "Flashing Numbers" Activity Sheet 1 or 2 (pages 125–126)
- 10 or 20 Unifix Cubes or other markers

For the teacher:

- Ten-Frame Cards 1–10 or 1–20 (pages 114–115)

## ◉ Overview

In this activity, students place Unifix Cubes in a ten-frame to show a set of objects that was flashed before them for a few seconds.

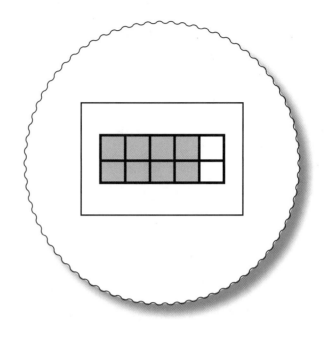

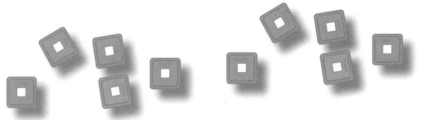

## Common Core State Standards

### Content Standards:

**Grade Level:** K

**Domain:** Counting and Cardinality (K.CC)

**Count to tell the number of objects.**

5. Count to answer "how many?" questions about as many as 20 things arranged in a line, a rectangular array, or a circle, or as many as 10 things in a scattered configuration; given a number from 1–20, count out that many objects.

### Practice Standards:

7. **Look for and make use of structure.**

   Kindergarten students observe dot patterns and ten-frame patterns for various numbers 1–10. With practice, they identify a quantity without counting by ones. This ability is called *subitization*.

# 📑 Presenting the Activity

1. Make copies of the Ten-Frame Cards, cut them out, and glue them to the center of white paper plates. Depending on your class, make a set from 1 to 10 or 1 to 20.

2. Distribute 10 (or 20) Unifix Cubes and Activity Sheet 1 or 2 to each student.

3. Say to the student(s):

   > 🗨 I am going to show you a set of dots for a few seconds. When I hide them, I want you to take your Unifix Cubes and cover the squares of your ten-frame on your activity sheet to show me the number of dots you saw.

4. You may need to demonstrate the activity with one Number Array Circle.

5. Allow time for students to complete the sample task.

6. Say to the student(s):

   > 🗨 After you have placed your Unifix Cubes, write the number in the blank beside the letter A.

   > Then, take the cubes off the frame and I will show you another circle.

7. Repeat the activity for all 10 or 20 Number Array Circles. (Note: The activity can be extended by having students show one more or one less than the number of dots.)

# ☑ Assessing Student Responses

The following questions will help you assess your students' responses to the activity:

- Did the student(s) correctly show the number of cubes corresponding to each Ten-Frame Card shown?

- Did the student(s) have difficulty with any particular number?

- Did the student(s) try to count out the number of filled squares shown?

# 10: Comparing, Comparing

## ⓘ Number of Students

Partner pairs

## ⊘ Materials

For each student:

- Ten-Frames Template (page 110)
- 10 two-color counters (red/yellow)
- Small paper bag

## ◈ Overview

In this activity, students compare two ten-frames using two-color counters to determine the larger number of objects.

## Common Core State Standards

### Content Standards:

**Grade Level:** K

**Domain:** Counting and Cardinality (K.CC)

**Compare numbers.**

6. Identify whether the number of objects in one group is greater than, less than, or equal to the number of objects in another group, e.g., by using matching and counting strategies.

### Practice Standards:

2. **Reason abstractly and quantitatively.**

   Students must make sense of the quantities on each of the ten-frames.

# ⊡ Presenting the Activity

1. Make copies of the Ten-Frames Template and distribute to each student.

2. Distribute small paper bags to each student with 10 two-color counters inside.

3. Determine which partner will be the "red" player and which partner will be the "yellow" player.

4. Say to the students:

   **❝** You will be working with a partner to compare the number of red counters you have to the number of yellow counters your partner has.

   First, shake your bag and then open it and let the counters fall gently on the table.

   The red player will only place and count the counters that land on the red side.

   The yellow player will only place and count the counters that land on the yellow side.

   For example, the red player has 3 red counters, and the yellow player has 5 yellow counters, like this:

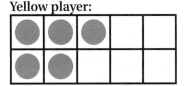

5. Say to the students:

   **❝** Now, decide whether the number of objects in the red group is greater than, less than, or equal to the number of objects in the yellow group.

   The player with the larger number of counters on his or her ten-frame wins the round.

6. Repeat the comparison, with partner pairs returning the counters to the bag to shake and place for round 2.

7. The comparisons continue with additional rounds as time allows.

# ⊘ Assessing Student Responses

The following questions will help you assess your students' responses to the activity:

• Did the student(s) correctly count the counters using one-to-one correspondence?

• Did the student(s) use a matching strategy to determine which color counter had more?

• Did the student(s) observe which ten-frame had more counters?

• Did the student(s) use terms such as *greater, more, less, fewer, equal to,* or *the same amount* to describe the comparison?

# 11: Ten in a Row

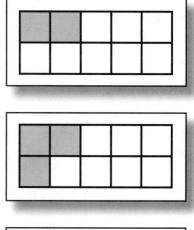

## ⓘ Number of Students

Small group

## ⊘ Materials

For each student:

• Ten-Frame Cards 1–20 (pages 114–115)

## ◈ Overview

In this game, students arrange their Ten-Frame Cards in order from 1 to 10 (or 1 to 20).

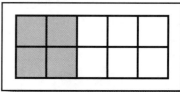

## Common Core State Standards

### Content Standards:

**Grade Level:** K

**Domain:** Counting and Cardinality (K.CC)

**Know number names and the count sequence.**

1. Count to 100 by ones and tens.

**Compare numbers.**

6. Identify whether the number of objects in one group is greater than, less than, or equal to the number of objects in another group, e.g., by using matching and counting strategies.

**Grade Level:** 1

**Domain:** Number and Operations in Base Ten (1.NBT)

**Understand place value.**

2. Understand that the two digits of a two-digit number represent amounts of tens and ones. Understand the following as special cases:

  a. 10 can be thought of as a bundle of ten ones — called a "ten."

  b. The numbers from 11 to 19 are composed of a ten and one, two, three, four, five, six, seven, eight, or nine ones.

### Practice Standards:

2. **Reason abstractly and quantitatively.**

   Kindergarten students make sense of quantities on ten-frames and attend to the ordering of numbers. In Grade 1, the thinking continues with numbers up to 20, with a focus on tens and ones.

3. **Construct viable arguments and critique the reasoning of others.**

   Students in Grades K and 1 are beginning their study of place value. In addition to the numbers 1 through 10, they are now focusing on numbers up to 20. By observing two different ten-frame cards, they must make an argument that explains why one representation is greater than, less than, or equal to another representation. During play, they also order the cards according to the number represented.

# 📖 Presenting the Activity

1.  Make copies of the Ten-Frame Cards, 1 to 10 or 1 to 20, depending on grade level. Cut them apart.

2.  Prepare one set of cards for each student in the group.

3.  Have students mix their set of cards thoroughly before playing.

4.  Say to the student(s):

    > 66 Each of you, place your set of Ten-Frame Cards facedown in front of you. Now, each of you draw a card and turn it over.
    >
    > Whoever has the greatest number starts.
    >
    > The student who starts draws another card from his/her deck and places it in the correct order to the left or right of the first card drawn.

5.  You may need to demonstrate how to play the first and second rounds.

6.  Say to the student(s):

    > 66 The student to the left now draws a card and places it to the left or right of his/her first card in the correct order.
    >
    > If you draw a card that you cannot play, you lose your turn. Place your card faceup in the discard pile.
    >
    > Now, the next player draws a card.
    >
    > The first player to get the numbers 1 to 10 (or 20) in a row is the winner.

7.  Allow time for students to complete the game.

# ✓ Assessing Student Responses

The following questions will help you assess your students' responses to the activity:

*   Did the student(s) compare the Ten-Frame Cards correctly?

*   Were representations of numbers in the teens difficult for students to compare? What did you observe?

*   What procedures Did the student(s) use to make comparisons? Did the student count the objects on the ten-frames first and then find the corresponding number? Did the student notice that one frame was completely filled and just count the markers on the second ten-frame?

# 12: Ten-Frames War

## (i) Number of Students

Partner pairs

## (/) Materials

For each student:

• Ten-Frame Cards (pages 114–115)

## (◆) Overview

In this activity, students compare two Ten-Frame Cards to determine the greater quantity.

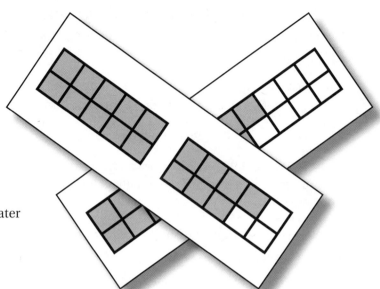

## Common Core State Standards

### Content Standards:

**Grade Level:** K

**Domain:** Counting and Cardinality (K.CC)

**Know number names and the count sequence.**

1. Count to 100 by ones and tens.

**Compare numbers.**

7. Compare two numbers between 1 and 10 presented as written numerals.

**Grade Level:** 1

**Domain:** Number and Operations in Base Ten (1.NBT)

**Understand place value.**

3. Compare two two-digit numbers based on meanings of the tens and ones digits, recording the results of comparisons with the symbols >, =, and <.

### Practice Standards:

2. **Reason abstractly and quantitatively.**

   Kindergarten students must be able to "transfer" a quantity represented on the Ten-Frame Cards to the corresponding quantity (1 to 10), and then write an appropriate symbolic comparison statement relating the two numbers, e.g., $a < b$, $a > b$, $a = b$. In Grade 1, the thinking continues with numbers up to 20, with a focus on tens.

3. **Construct viable arguments and critique the reasoning of others.**

   Students in Grades K and 1 are beginning their study of place value. In addition to the numbers 1 to 10, they are now focusing on numbers up to 20. In comparing two different Ten-Frame Cards, they must argue why one representation is greater than, less than, or equal to another representation.

# ⬚ Presenting the Activity

1. Make copies of the Ten-Frame Cards using two colors of cardstock. Cut them apart.

2. Distribute the two sets of cards to the student pairs. Each student gets his or her own color.

3. Say to the student(s):

   **❝** Place your set of Ten-Frame Cards facedown in front of you. Now, each one of you, turn over a card.

   Whoever has the greater number wins the round and takes the cards.

4. You may need to demonstrate how to play a round.

5. Say to the student(s):

   **❝** For each round, write a number sentence that relates the two numbers. For example, if the two numbers showing are 8 and 13, then write $13 > 8$ on your paper.

6. Say to the student(s):

   **❝** If you have the same quantity showing, turn over another card. Whoever has the greater number wins all of the cards.

   Continue turning over cards for each round until you have no more cards.

   The winner of Ten-Frames War is the player with more cards.

7. Allow time for students to complete the game.

# ⦿ Assessing Student Responses

The following questions will help you assess your students' responses to the activity:

- Did the student(s) compare the Ten-Frame Cards correctly?

- Were representations of numbers in the teens difficult for students to compare? What did you observe?

- What procedure did the student(s) use to make comparisons? Did the student count the objects on the ten-frames before naming the corresponding number? Did the student notice that one frame was completely filled and just count the markers on the second ten-frame?

- Did the student(s) write correct number sentences using "greater than" or "less than" symbols?

# 13: Target Number Addition Roll

## ⓘ Number of Students

Partner pairs

## ⊘ Materials

For each student:

- 2 ten-frames or Ten-Frames Template (page 110)

For each pair of students:

- Number Cards 2–12 (pages 117–118)
- Assortment of colored Unifix Cubes
- Six-sided number cube (1–6)

## ◈ Overview

In this activity, a target number is selected. Students will represent addition by combining Unifix Cubes on one or two ten-frames to determine whether they have reached the target number.

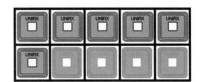

## Common Core State Standards

**Content Standards:**

**Grade Level:** K

**Domain:** Operations and Algebraic Thinking (K.OA)

**Understand addition as putting together and adding to, and understand subtraction as taking apart and taking from.**

1. Represent addition and subtraction with objects, fingers, mental images, drawings, sounds (e.g., claps), acting out situations, verbal explanations, expressions, or equations.

**Practice Standards:**

2. **Reason abstractly and quantitatively.**

   Students must make sense of the quantities involved in the activity.

4. **Model with mathematics.**

   Students will use Unifix Cubes to model addition.

# Presenting the Activity

1. Make copies of the Number Cards for partner pairs.

2. Make a copy of the Ten-Frames Template for each student.

3. Group students in partner pairs.

4. Distribute Unifix Cubes and 1–6 number cube to partner pairs.

5. Say to the students:

   66 Shuffle the Number Cards and place them facedown between you and your partner.

   Player 1, draw the top card and show it to your partner. This number becomes the target number for Player 2.

   For example, suppose the card drawn is the number 10. Player 2 will toss the number cube two times.

   Each time the number cube is tossed, Player 2 will count Unifix Cubes to match the number tossed and place them on his or her ten-frame(s).

   For example, if the first roll lands on the number 6, Player 2 places six cubes of the same color on the frame. If the second roll is also a 6, Player 2 then adds 6 more cubes of a different color to the ten-frames, like this:

   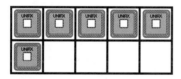

   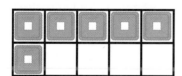

6. Say to the students:

   66 Now, Player 2 will combine the cubes on the ten-frames. Player 2 should notice the total as one ten and two ones, or 12.

   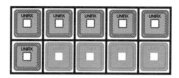

   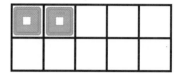

7. Say to the students:

   66 Player 2, look at selected target number of (10). Is this number a match? If not, how close to (10) is the number you have?

   Player 2 may state, "My number is 2 more than 10."

8. The activity continues with Player 2 selecting a target number for Player 1. The above process is repeated.

## ⊙ Assessing Student Responses

The following questions will help you assess your students' responses to the activity:

- Did the student(s) use the appropriate terminology such as *added to, joined, equals,* etc.?

- Did the student(s) understand the concept of addition?

- Did the student(s) use a strategy for combining the sets, i.e., doubles?

- Could the student(s) explain how close the target number was?

# 14: 1 Scoop, 2 Scoops, 3 Scoops

## ⓘ Number of Students

Partner pairs

## ⊘ Materials

For each student:

- Unifix Ten-Frame Trains (commercially available)
- 20 Unifix Cubes

## ◈ Overview

In this activity, partner pairs of students will "scoop" handfuls of Unifix Cubes with the purpose of joining (adding) the handfuls of cubes together to create a Unifix train.

## Common Core State Standards

### Content Standards:

**Grade Level:** K

**Domain:** Operations and Algebraic Thinking (K.OA)

**Understand addition as putting together and adding to, and understand subtraction as taking apart and taking from.**

1. Represent addition and subtraction with objects, fingers, mental images, drawings, sounds (e.g., claps), acting out situations, verbal explanations, expressions, or equations.

### Practice Standards:

2. **Reason abstractly and quantitatively.**

   Students must make sense of the quantities involved in the activity.

4. **Model with mathematics.**

   Students will use Unifix Cubes to model addition.

# Presenting the Activity

1. Distribute 20 cubes to each student.

2. Group the students into partner pairs.

3. Say to the students:

   > Student 1, scoop one handful of Unifix Cubes, and count the cubes as you place them on your ten-frame train.
   >
   > Student 1, now state the number of cubes you placed (for example, "6").
   >
   > Student 2, scoop one handful of Unifix Cubes, and count the cubes as you place them on your ten-frame train.
   >
   > Student 2, state the number of cubes you placed (for example, "5").
   >
   > Student pairs, join your two trains together and state the number of cubes each of you placed, such as "6 and 5."
   >
   > Student pairs, add (6) cubes and (5) cubes.
   >
   > Now explain your strategy for finding the total.

4. Round 2 begins with the partner pairs each scooping **two** handfuls of cubes.

5. Say to the students:

   > Student 1, count both handfuls of your cubes (for example, "9") and place them on your ten-frame train.
   >
   > Student 2, do the same (for example, "8").
   >
   > Student pairs, join both trains together to find the total number of cubes.
   >
   > Explain your strategy for finding the total.

6. Finally, the partner pairs each scoop **three** handfuls of cubes and repeat the process described above.

7. Say to the students:

   > Student 1, count all three handfuls of your cubes (for example, "3 + 2 + 5 = 10") and place them on your ten-frame train.
   >
   > Student 2, count all three handfuls of your cubes (for example, "2 + 3 + 4 = 9") and place them on your ten-frame train.
   >
   > Student pairs, join both trains together to find the total number of cubes (for example, 10 + 9 = 19).
   >
   > Now explain the strategy you used for finding the total.

# Assessing Student Responses

The following questions will help you assess your students' responses to the activity:

- Did the student(s) use the appropriate terminology, such as *added to*, *joined*, *equals*, and so on?

- Did the student(s) understand the concept of addition?

- Did the student(s) use strategies for combining the sets?

# 15: Finger Flash

## (i) Number of Students

Entire class

## (∅) Materials

For each student:
- 2 ten-frames or Ten-Frames Template (page 110)
- 10 Unifix Cubes

## (◈) Overview

In this activity, students respond to two visual addends (fingers) and find the sum using cubes on a ten-frame.

## Common Core State Standards

### Content Standards:

**Grade Level:** K

**Domain:** Operations and Algebraic Thinking (K.OA)

**Understand addition as putting together and adding to, and understand subtraction as taking apart and taking from.**

1. Represent addition and subtraction with objects, fingers, mental images, drawings, sounds (e.g., claps), acting out situations, verbal explanations, expressions, or equations.

2. Solve addition and subtraction word problems, and add and subtract within 10, e.g., by using objects or drawings to represent the problem.

### Practice Standards:

2. **Reason abstractly and quantitatively.**

   Students visualize two different quantities, make sense of them, and then manipulate objects to find a sum.

# ⓐ Presenting the Activity

1. Make copies of the Ten-Frames Template on card stock. Commercial ten-frames are also available.

2. Distribute 10 Unifix Cubes and a ten-frame to each student.

3. Say to the student(s):

   **❝** I am going to hold up fingers on each hand.

   I want you to place Unifix Cubes on your ten-frames to show me the total number of fingers I'm holding up.

   When you finish, I want you to write a number sentence that shows what you did.

4. You may need to demonstrate the activity, showing students how to write the corresponding number sentence.

5. Repeat the activity several times with various finger configurations.

# ⓐ Assessing Student Responses

The following questions will help you assess your students' responses to the activity:

- Did the student(s) correctly model the set-up and solution to each Finger Flash situation?

- Did the student(s) write the correct addition number sentence? If not, what type of error was present?

- Did the student(s) find the correct sum?

- Did you observe any patterns as the student(s) went from the visual images to the concrete objects to the symbolic notation?

# 16: Make My Number

## ⓘ Number of Students

Partner pairs

## ⊘ Materials

For each student:

• 2 two ten-frames or Ten-frames Template (page 110)

For each pair of students:

• Number Cards 2–12 (page 117–118)
• 6-sided number cube or die
• Assortment of colored Unifix Cubes

## ◈ Overview

In this activity, a target number is selected.
Students will represent addition by joining
Unifix Cubes on a ten-frame to determine if
they have reached the target number.

## Common Core State Standards

### Content Standards:

**Grade Level:** K

**Domain:** Operations and Algebraic Thinking (K.OA)

**Understand addition as putting together and adding to, and understand subtraction as taking apart and taking from.**

1. Represent addition and subtraction with objects,
   fingers, mental images, drawings, sounds (e.g.,
   claps), acting out situations, verbal explanations,
   expressions, or equations.

### Practice Standards:

2. **Reason abstractly and quantitatively.**

   Students must make sense of the quantities
   involved in the activity.

4. **Model with mathematics.**

   Students will use Unifix Cubes to model addition.

# ⊡ Presenting the Activity

1. Group students to work in partner pairs.

2. Say to the students:

   ❝ Shuffle the Number Cards and place them facedown in a pile.

   To start, Player 1 will draw the top card and show it to your partner.

   This number becomes the target number for Player 2. For example, the card drawn is the number 10.

3. Say to the students:

   ❝ Player 2 will toss the number cube two times.

   Each time the number cube is tossed, Player 2 will count Unifix Cubes to match the number tossed and place them on one of the ten-frames.

   For example, the first toss shows the number 6. Player 2 places six cubes of the same color on the frame.

   The second toss is also a 6. Player 2 then places six more cubes of a different color to the other ten-frame, like this:

   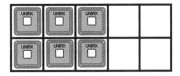 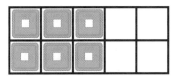

4. Say to the students:

   ❝ Player 2, now combine the cubes on the two ten-frames (as shown) to demonstrate the total as "one ten and two ones, or 12."

   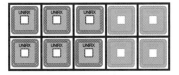 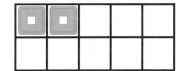

5. Say to the students:

   ❝ Player 2, look at the target number (10). Is your number a match? If not, how close is your number? (Player 2 may state, "My number is 2 more than 10.")

6. The activity continues with Player 2 selecting a target number for Player 1, with the process repeated as above.

# ⊙ Assessing Student Responses

The following questions will help you assess your students' responses to the activity:

- Did the student(s) use the appropriate terminology, such as *added to, joined, equals,* etc.?

- Did the student(s) understand the concept of addition?

- Did the student(s) use a strategy for combining the sets, i.e., doubles?

- Can the student(s) explain how close the target number is?

# 17: Take Away

## ⓘ Number of Students

Individuals or partner pairs

## ⊘ Materials

For each pair of students:

• Take-Away Cards (page 127)

For each student:

• "Take Away" Activity Sheet 1 or 2 (pages 128–129)

• 10 Unifix Cubes of one color, or other markers

## ◈ Overview

In this activity, students first place 10 Unifix Cubes or other markers in a ten-frame, and then remove or "take away" a specific number of cubes. The second "Take Away" activity sheet can be used for subtraction number sentences, beginning with a number other than 10.

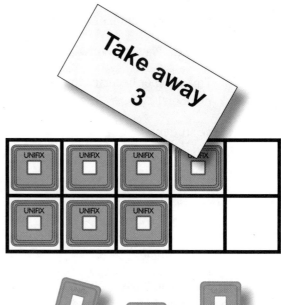

$$10 - 3 = 7$$

---

## Common Core State Standards

### Content Standards:

**Grade Level:** K

**Domain:** Operations and Algebraic Thinking (K.OA)

**Understand addition as putting together and adding to, and understand subtraction as taking apart and taking from.**

1.  Solve addition and subtraction word problems, and add or subtract within 10, e.g., by using objects or drawings to represent the problem.

### Practice Standards:

4.  **Model with mathematics.**

    Students are using manipulatives to model basic subtraction facts within 10. From the visual representations they create on the "Take Away" activity sheet, they are writing the corresponding subtraction equation.

7.  **Look for and make use of structure.**

    As students continue making 10 in this activity, they begin to understand basic patterns about fact families for addition and subtraction, such as $2 + 8 = 8 + 2$, along with $10 - 2 = 8$ and $10 - 8 = 2$.

# ⬛ Presenting the Activity

1. Make copies of the Take-Away Cards on card stock and cut them apart.

2. Distribute 10 Unifix Cubes of one color, or other markers, and a set of Take-Away Cards to each student or pair.

3. Say to the student(s):

   66 Place all 10 of your Unifix Cubes on the ten-frame.

4. You may need to demonstrate the activity with one card.

5. Allow time for students to complete the task.

6. Say to the student(s):

   66 Now, draw a Take-Away Card from the pile. Take away that number of cubes from your ten-frame.

7. Repeat the activity for all 10 Take-Away Cards.

8. For each Take-Away Card drawn, say to student(s):

   66 Write the number from the card on the first line, and then write the number of cubes that remain on the second line: $10 - 4 = 6$.

9. For each number sentence, say to student(s):

   Tell me the number sentence you wrote.

# ✓ Assessing Student Responses

The following questions will help you assess your students' responses to the activity:

- Did the student(s) correctly remove the number of cubes for each Take-Away Card?

- Did the student(s) determine the correct number of remaining cubes?

- What procedure did the student(s) use to determine the difference? Did the student count one by one the remaining cubes in the ten-frame? Did the student "see" and then state the remaining number of cubes?

- Did the student have any difficulty completing the subtraction number sentences on the activity sheet?

- Did the student(s) notice or communicate any patterns, such as $10 - 3 = 7$ and $10 - 7 = 3$?

# 18: My Missing Number of Cubes

## (i) Number of Students

Partner pairs

## (/) Materials

For each student:

• "My Missing Number" Recording Sheet (page 130)

For each pair of students:

• Number Cards 1–10, 1 set (pages 117–118)
• 20 Unifix Cubes
• Blank sheet of 8.5 × 11 in. paper

## (◆) Overview

In this activity, students will use Unifix Cubes to model how a number can be decomposed. Students will also break apart the number in another way and record by a drawing or equation.

## Common Core State Standards

### Content Standards:

**Grade Level:** K

**Domain:** Operations and Algebraic Thinking (K.OA)

**Understand addition as putting together and adding to, and understand subtraction as taking apart and taking from.**

3. Decompose numbers less than or equal to 10 into pairs in more than one way, e.g., by using objects or drawings, and record each decomposition by a drawing or equation (e.g., 5 = 2 + 3 and 5 = 4 + 1).

### Practice Standards:

2. **Reason abstractly and quantitatively.**

   Students must make sense of the quantity involved in each number.

4. **Model with mathematics.**

   Students are using manipulatives to model decomposition of numbers.

# 🗂 Presenting the Activity

1. Make copies of the Number Cards (1–10) on card stock and cut them apart.

2. Make copies of the recording page for each student and distribute.

3. Distribute Unfix Cubes to each pair of students.

4. Say to the students:

   💬 Shuffle the number cards and place them facedown between each of you.

   Decide who will be Player 1 and who will be Player 2 by choosing a card from the Number Card pile. The player with the higher number begins.

   Place the cards back in the deck.

   Player 1 takes the top card from the deck, looks at the number, and places it facedown between the players.

   Player 2 closes his or her eyes.

   Player 1 quickly counts out the same number of Unifix Cubes as the number on the card, then hides some of the cubes under the sheet of paper.

   For example, if Player 1 draws the number 6, he/she could hide two cubes under the paper and show four cubes, like this:

5. Say to the students:

   💬 Now Player 2 opens his/her eyes.

   Using this example, Player 1 states: "My number is six. How many cubes are hidden?"

   Player 2 tells the number of cubes hidden under the paper, then records this on the recording page by writing a number sentence (for example, $4 + 2 = 6$) or drawing a picture.

   Player 2 then provides another way to make 6.

6. Repeat the process with Player 2 taking a turn hiding cubes for Player 1.

## ⊘ Assessing Student Responses

The following questions will help you assess your students' responses to the activity:

- Did the student(s) correctly draw the picture or write the number sentence on the recording page?

- Did the student(s) show an additional decomposition for the number?

- Are any specific number combinations difficult for students?

**"My Missing Number of Cubes" Recording Sheet**

| My number is: 6 | I see 4 cubes. | 2 cubes are hiding. |
|---|---|---|
| **Show this with cubes:** | | |

    $+$   $= 6$

# 19: Another Way

## (i) Number of Students

Individuals or partner pairs

## (✓) Materials

For each student:

- "Another Way" Activity Sheet (page 131)
- 20 Unifix Cubes (or other markers), 10 of one color and 10 of a different color
- Crayons, pencil

For each group:

- Number Cards 1–10 (pages 117–118)

## (◈) Overview

In this activity, students place two colors of Unifix Cubes in a ten-frame to show two different addends for a specific sum.

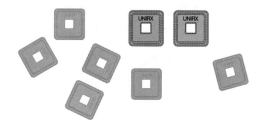

## Common Core State Standards

### Content Standards:

**Grade Level:** K

**Domain:** Counting and Cardinality (K.CC)

**Count to tell the number of objects.**

4. Understand the relationship between numbers and quantities; connect counting to cardinality.

   c. Understand that each successive number name refers to a quantity that is one larger.

**Domain:** Operations and Algebraic Thinking (K.OA)

**Understand addition as putting together and adding to, and understand subtraction as taking apart and taking from.**

2. Solve addition and subtraction word problems, and add or subtract within 10, e.g., by using objects or drawings to represent the problem.

### Practice Standards:

1. **Make sense of problems and persevere in solving them.**

   Given a specific sum, students use concrete objects to decompose the number into two addends in more than one way. They begin to analyze the problem: Having found one decomposition, for example, 4 + 5 = 9, another can be found by increasing (decreasing) one addend and decreasing (increasing) the other addend, for example, 3 + 6 = 9 or 5 + 4 = 9.

# Mathematical Note:

As students progress in this activity, they will notice a pattern in the number of possible ways to show a particular sum. The number varies, depending on whether or not 0 is included. Below are the decompositions up to a sum of 10:

| 2 | 3 | 4 | 5 | 6 | 7 | 8 | 9 | 10 |
|---|---|---|---|---|---|---|---|---|
| 1 + 1 | 1 + 2 | 1 + 3 | 1 + 4 | 1 + 5 | 1 + 6 | 1 + 7 | 1 + 8 | 1 + 9 |
| | 2 + 1 | 2 + 2 | 2 + 3 | 2 + 4 | 2 + 5 | 2 + 6 | 2 + 7 | 2 + 8 |
| | | 3 + 1 | 3 + 2 | 3 + 3 | 3 + 4 | 3 + 5 | 3 + 6 | 3 + 7 |
| | | | 4 + 1 | 4 + 2 | 4 + 3 | 4 + 4 | 4 + 5 | 4 + 6 |
| | | | | 5 + 1 | 5 + 2 | 5 + 3 | 5 + 4 | 5 + 5 |
| | | | | | 6 + 1 | 6 + 2 | 6 + 3 | 6 + 4 |
| | | | | | | 7 + 1 | 7 + 2 | 7 + 3 |
| | | | | | | | 8 + 1 | 8 + 2 |
| | | | | | | | | 9 + 1 |

The number of decompositions is one less than the specific sum. For example, a sum of 5 has 4 decompositions and a sum of 8 has 7 decompositions.

If 0 is included as an addend, then the number of decompositions is one more than the specific sum.

---

## ⊡ Presenting the Activity

1. Make a copy of the Number Cards 1–10 on card stock and cut them apart.

2. Copy and distribute the "Another Way" Activity Sheet to each student.

3. Distribute Unifix Cubes to each student.

4. Show students a Number Card and write the sum at the top of each student's sheet, or have the students write the sum at the top of their sheets.

5. Say to the student(s):

   **❝** The number on the card (or at the top of your sheet) is the sum of two numbers. Use two different colors of Unifix Cubes to show me how you might get this sum.

6. You may need to demonstrate the activity with one card and write the corresponding decomposition.

7. Allow time for students to complete the task.

8. Say to the student(s):

   **❝** Now, shade in the ten-frame with your crayons to show what you just found.

When you finish, write your answer on the blanks. Then, see if you can find another way to show the sum.

9. Have students repeat the activity until you observe that all decompositions have been found.

## ⊘ Assessing Student Responses

The following questions will help you assess your students' responses to the activity:

- Did the student(s) find all the decompositions for a particular sum?

- Did the student(s) have difficulty with any particular number?

- After finding one decomposition, did the student(s) use any particular procedure to find additional decompositions?

- Did the student(s) count the number of decompositions to look for a pattern?

# 20: Make Ten

## ⓘ Number of Students

Individual, small group, or entire class

## ⊘ Materials

For each student:

- "Make Ten" Activity Sheet (page 132)
- 18 Unifix Cubes (or other markers), 9 each of two different colors

For each group:

- Number Cards 1–9 (page 117)

## ◈ Overview

In this activity, students place Unifix Cubes or other markers in a ten-frame to make 10.

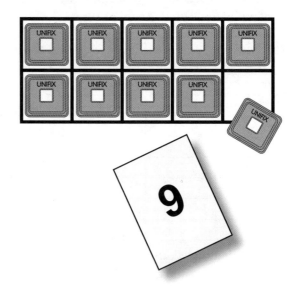

$$9 + 1 = 10$$

## Common Core State Standards

### Content Standards:

**Grade Level:** K

**Domain:** Operations and Algebraic Thinking (K.OA)

**Understand addition as putting together and adding to, and understand subtraction as taking apart and taking from.**

4. For any number from 1 to 9, find the number that makes 10 when added to the given number, e.g., by using objects or drawings, and record the answer with a drawing or equation.

### Practice Standards:

4. **Model with mathematics.**

   Students are using manipulatives to model basic addition facts to 10. From the visual representation they create on the ten-frame activity sheet, they are writing the corresponding addition equation.

7. **Look for and make use of structure.**

   As students continue making 10 in this activity, they begin to notice patterns, such as 2 + 8 is the same as 8 + 2. The addends are just in a different order.

# ⓘ Presenting the Activity

1.  Make copies of the Number Cards 1–9 on card stock and cut them apart.

2.  Distribute the Unifix Cubes or markers to each student.

3.  Say to the student(s):

    **❝** Draw a Number Card. Put that number of Unifix Cubes on your ten-frame using one color.

4.  You may need to demonstrate the activity with one card.

5.  Allow time for students to complete the task.

6.  Say to the student(s):

    **❝** Now, how many more cubes do you need to make 10? Use the other color of cubes to fill the ten-frame.

7.  Repeat the activity for all 9 Number Cards.

8.  For each Number Card you show, say to the student(s):

    **❝** Write the number I showed you in the first space, and then write the number that will make 10 in the second space—for example, 6 + 4 = 10.

9.  For each number sentence the students record, say:

    **❝** Tell me the number sentence you wrote.

# ⊘ Assessing Student Responses

The following questions will help you assess your students' responses to the activity:

*   Did the student(s) place the correct number of cubes for each number shown?

*   Did the student(s) determine the correct number of cubes to make 10?

*   What procedure did the student(s) use to determine what makes 10? Did the student count the remaining squares in the ten-frame? Did the student count on from the number shown—for example, 8, 9, 10, so 8 + 2 = 10?

*   Did the student(s) have any difficulty completing the number sentences on the activity sheet?

*   Did the student(s) notice any patterns, such as 4 + 6 = 6 + 4?

# 21: Target Ten

## (i) Number of Students

Partner pairs

## (/) Materials

For each pair of students:

• Ten-Frame Cards 1–10 (page 114)

## (◆) Overview

In this activity, students pair two Ten-Frame Cards that make a sum of 10.

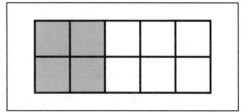

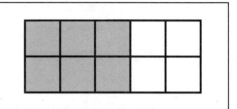

$$4 + 6 = 10$$

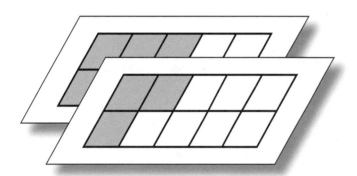

---

## Common Core State Standards

### Content Standards:

**Grade Level:** K

**Domain:** Operations and Algebraic Thinking (K.OA)

**Understand addition as putting together and adding to, and understand subtraction as taking apart and taking from.**

4. For any number from 1 to 9, find the number that makes 10 when added to the given number, e.g., by using objects or drawings, and record the answer with a drawing or equation.

### Practice Standards:

4. **Model with mathematics.**

Students are using manipulatives to model basic addition facts to 10. The representations of numbers on the ten-frames provide visual images of numbers that "make 10."

7. **Look for and make use of structure.**

As students continue making 10 in this activity, they begin to notice patterns, such as 3 + 7 is the same as 7 + 3.

---

# (📑) Presenting the Activity

1. Make copies of the Ten-Frame Cards on card stock and cut them apart.

2. Distribute a set of Ten-Frame Cards to each pair of students.

3. Say to the students:

   (🗣) Mix up the Ten-Frame Cards and then place them faceup in front of both of you.

   One of you starts by finding two cards that have a sum of 10 shaded squares.

   When you find a pair, pick them up and place them beside you.

   Then it's your partner's turn to find two cards that have a sum of 10.

   Keep playing until all the cards are paired.

   Each of you will end up with two pairs of cards, with one card left over.

4. You may need to demonstrate the activity with one card.

5. Allow time for students to complete the task.

6. For each pair of Ten-Frame Cards drawn, say to the student(s):

   (🗣) Write a number sentence that shows the two cards you drew—for example, $6 + 4 = 10$.

7. For each number sentence the students write, say:

   (🗣) Tell me the number sentence you wrote.

# (✓) Assessing Student Responses

The following questions will help you assess your students' responses to the activity:

- Did the student(s) correctly pair the Ten-Frame Cards, leaving the card with five shaded squares?

- Did the student(s) write the correct number sentences for each pair?

- What procedure did the student(s) use to determine the Ten-Frame Cards that make 10? Did the student(s) count the shaded squares in each ten-frame? Did they count on from one Ten-Frame Card to another to make the pair—for example, 8, 9, 10, so $8 + 2 = 10$?

# 22: Spin to Win

## ⓘ Number of Students

Partner pairs

## ⊘ Materials

For each student:

- 2 ten-frames or Ten-Frames Template (page 110)
- "Spin to Win" Recording Sheet (page 134)
- Paper clip and pencil to use with spinner

For each pair:

- "Spin to Win" Spinner (page 133)
- 40 Unifix Cubes

## ◈ Overview

In this activity, students work with the place value of teen numbers by spinning numbers and placing Unifix Cubes on ten-frames. Students should be able to state that "teen" numbers mean "one ten and some ones."

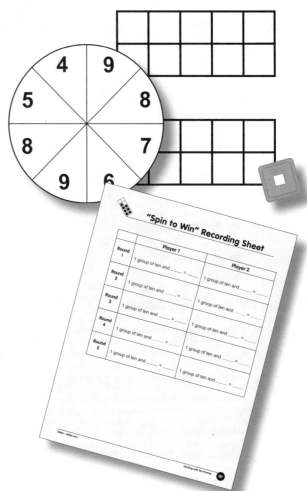

## Common Core State Standards

### Content Standards:

**Grade Level:** K

**Domain:** Number and Operations in Base Ten (K.NBT)

**Work with numbers 11–19 to gain foundations for place value.**

1. Compose and decompose numbers from 11 to 19 into ten ones and some further ones, e.g., by using objects or drawings, and record each composition or decomposition by a drawing or equation (e.g., $18 = 10 + 8$); understand that these numbers are composed of ten ones and one, two, three, four, five, six, seven, eight, or nine ones.

### Practice Standards:

2. **Reason abstractly and quantitatively.**

   Students must make sense of the quantity in each grouping of cubes.

7. **Look for and make use of structure.**

   Students should recognize the pattern that exists in the teen numbers; every teen number is written with a "1" and ends with the digit that is said first.

# 📑 Presenting the Activity

1. Reproduce and distribute one "Spin to Win" Recording Sheet and Spinner Sheet per partner pair.

2. Distribute a pencil to each student and a paper clip to use for the spinner.

3. Distribute 2 ten-frames per student.

4. Distribute 40 Unifix Cubes per partner pair.

5. Say to the students:

   (66) On your turn, each of you will spin a number and place that number of cubes on your ten-frames.

   Player 1 will spin first. For example, if Player 1 spins 9, he/she will place nine cubes on his/her ten-frame, like this:

6. Say to the students:

   (66) Player 2 will spin next. If Player 2 lands on the number 6, for example, he/she will place six cubes.

   Player 1, you will spin a second time to add to your previous total. For example, if you land on the number 5, you will add five more cubes to the number of cubes you already have to display 14 cubes. It will look like this:

   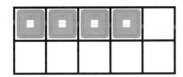

7. Say to the students:

   (66) Player 2, you will also spin to add to your previous total.

   Now both players count the number of cubes on your ten-frames and record the number as "1 group of ten and _____ones = _____."

   The player with the greater number wins the round.

   | Player 1 | |
   | --- | --- |
   | **Round 1** | 1 group of ten and __4__ = __14__ |

# ✓ Assessing Student Responses

The following questions will help you assess your students' responses to the activity.

- Did the student(s) interpret and express teen numbers as "ten plus some ones"?

- Students should recognize the pattern that exists in the teen numbers; every teen number is written with a 1 (representing one ten) and ends with the digit that is stated first.

- Did the student(s) verbally count 14 ("four . . . teen") and notice the counting pattern is the reverse of "one ten and four ones"?

- Did the student(s) notice the numbers 11 and 12 do not follow the pattern?

- Did the student(s) use a counting strategy, i.e., counting on or making a ten when adding the Unifix Cubes together?

# 23: Spin It, Show It

### ⓘ Number of Students

Partner pairs

### ⊘ Materials

For each student:
- 2 ten-frames or Ten-Frames Template (page 110)
- 20 two-color counters

For each pair of students:
- Tens and Ones Place Value Cards (page 135)
- 11–19 Spinner (page 136)
- Paper clip and pencil to use with the spinner

### ◈ Overview

In this activity, students use the 11–19 Spinner Sheet to spin a "teen" number and match the number to a Tens and Ones Place Value Card. Students will also display the number using two-color counters and ten-frames.

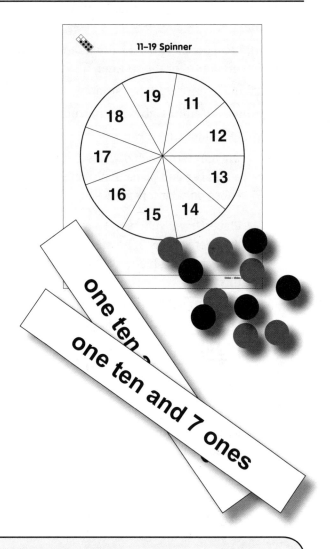

## Common Core State Standards

### Content Standards:

**Grade Level:** K

**Domain:** Number and Operations in Base Ten (K.NBT)

**Work with numbers 11–19 to gain foundations for place value.**

1. Compose and decompose numbers from 11 to 19 into ten ones and some further ones, e.g., by using objects or drawings, and record each composition or decomposition by a drawing or equation (e.g., $18 = 10 + 8$); understand that these numbers are composed of ten ones and one, two, three, four, five, six, seven, eight, or nine ones.

### Practice Standards:

2. **Reason abstractly and quantitatively.**

   Students must make sense of the quantity in each grouping of cubes.

7. **Look for and make use of structure.**

   Students should recognize the pattern that exists in the teen numbers; every teen number is written with a "1" and ends with the digit that is said first.

# 🔖 Presenting the Activity

1.  Reproduce the 11–19 Spinner Sheet.

2.  Reproduce and cut apart the Tens and Ones Place Value Cards.

3.  Distribute two-color counters to each player.

4.  Distribute 2 ten-frames, or copy and distribute the Ten-Frames Template, to each player.

5.  Distribute one 11–19 Spinner Sheet and paper clip/pencil per partner pair.

6.  Say to students:

    ❝ I will deal out the cards to you and your partner.

    You will each receive 5 cards. Place them faceup in front of you.

    Player 1 will spin the spinner and land on a number between 10 and 20. For example, suppose Player 1 lands on 13. Both players will look at their own cards to see who has the Place Value Card showing the match for the number 13:

    | **one ten and 3 ones** |
    |---|

    Whichever player has the card will say, "I have one ten and three ones," and then must show what one ten and three ones looks like using the two-color counters and ten-frames.

    Both players must agree that the ten-frame displays 13. If correct, the player who has the "one ten and 3 ones" card will put the card in the discard pile.

    The first player to discard all five of his/her Place Value Cards is the winner.

# ◉ Assessing Student Responses

The following questions will help you assess your students' responses to the activity.

*   Did the student(s) express teen numbers as "ten plus some ones"?

*   Did the student(s) find the pattern that exists in the teen number? (Every teen number is written with a 1 and ends with the digit that is stated first.)

*   Did the student(s) verbally count 14 (four ... teen) and notice the counting pattern is backward from one ten and 4 ones?

*   Did the student(s) notice that the numbers 11 and 12 do not follow the pattern?

*   Did the student(s) use a counting strategy when displaying two-color counters on the ten-frames?

# 24: Place Value Game

## (i) Number of Students

Entire class

## (∕) Materials

For each student:

- Place Value Game Boards (pages 137–140)
- 12 game markers or chips
- 2 ten-frames or Ten-Frames Template (optional) (page 110)
- Unifix Cubes (optional)

For the caller:

- Place Value Caller's Cards (page 141)

## (✦) Overview

In this activity, students locate the place value of teen numbers, applying the concept that "teen" numbers mean "one ten and some ones."

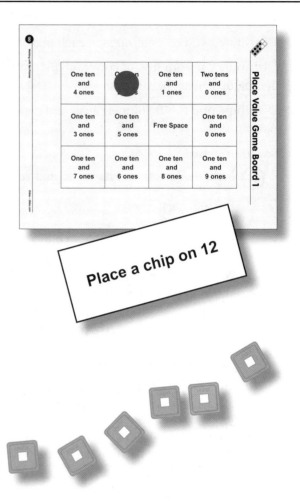

Place a chip on 12

---

## Common Core State Standards

### Content Standards:

**Grade Level:** K

**Domain:** Number and Operations in Base Ten (K.NBT)

**Work with numbers 11–19 to gain foundations for place value.**

1. Compose and decompose numbers from 11 to 19 into ten ones and some further ones, e.g., by using objects or drawings, and record each composition or decomposition by a drawing or equation (e.g., $18 = 10 + 8$); understand that these numbers are composed of ten ones and one, two, three, four, five, six, seven, eight, or nine ones.

### Practice Standards:

2. **Reason abstractly and quantitatively.**

   Students must make sense of the quantity in each grouping of cubes.

7. **Look for and make use of structure.**

   Students should recognize the pattern that exists in the teen numbers; every teen number is written with a "1" and ends with the digit that is said first.

# 🔲 Presenting the Activity

1. Reproduce the Place Value Game Boards for each student. (There are 4 different boards.) Distribute one board to each student.

2. Reproduce and cut apart the Place Value Cards for the leader.

3. Distribute 12 chips or markers to each student.

4. Say to the students:

   > 66 Everyone will start by placing a chip on the free space on their board.
   >
   > I will randomly select a Place Value Card and read it out loud.
   >
   > Pick up one chip and place it on the board to match the number I read.
   >
   > The goal is to cover all the spaces on your board. You may use ten-frames and Unifix Cubes, if you need to.

# ⊙ Assessing Student Responses

The following questions will help you assess your students' responses to the activity:

- Did the student(s) interpret teen numbers as "ten plus some ones"?

- Did the student(s) recognize the pattern that exists in the teen numbers: every written teen number starts with a 1 (representing one ten) and ends with the digit that is stated first—for example, four teen or seven teen.

- Did the student(s) notice that the counting pattern is backward from "one ten and four ones"?

- Did the student(s) notice that the numbers 11 and 12 do not follow the pattern?

# 25: More Than Ten

## ⓘ Number of Students

Entire class

## ⊘ Materials

For each student:
- "More Than Ten" Activity Sheet (page142)
- 20 Unifix Cubes

For the teacher:
- Number Cards 11–20 (pages 118–119)

## ⊕ Overview

In this activity, students are shown a number between 11 and 20. They decompose the number into a group of 10 and remaining ones. They place Unifix Cubes in two ten-frames to show the decomposition and then write a number sentence that communicates the decomposition.

## Common Core State Standards

### Content Standards:

**Grade Level:** K

**Domain:** Number and Operations in Base Ten (K.NBT)

**Work with numbers 11–19 to gain foundations for place value.**

1. Compose and decompose numbers from 11 to 19 into ten ones and some further ones, e.g., by using objects or drawings, and record each composition or decomposition by a drawing or equation (e.g., $18 = 10 + 8$); understand that these numbers are composed of ten ones and one, two, three, four, five, six, seven, eight, or nine ones.

### Practice Standards:

4. **Model with mathematics.**

   As students begin their number experiences, they use manipulatives to show numbers greater than 10.

7. **Look for and make use of structure.**

   Kindergarten students learn that any whole number greater than 10 can be decomposed into groups of 10 and remaining ones. This understanding is critical for understanding operations on whole numbers.

# Presenting the Activity

1. Make copies of the Number Cards 11–20 on card stock and cut them apart.

2. Distribute 20 Unifix Cubes and a "More Than Ten" Activity Sheet to each student.

3. Say to the students:

   *I am going to show you a Number Card. Take your cubes and place them on your ten-frames to show the number as a group of 10 and some ones.*

4. You may need to demonstrate the activity with one card.

5. Allow time for students to complete the task.

6. Repeat the activity for each Number Card.

7. For each Number Card you show, say to students:

   *Write a number sentence on your paper showing how the number contains a group of 10 and some ones.*

   *When you finish writing your number sentence, remove your cubes from the ten-frames.*

**Note:** For many Grade 1 students, the activity will be simple. It can be extended by including additional ten-frames and using numbers greater than 20.

# Assessing Student Responses

The following questions will help you assess your students' responses to the activity:

- Did the student(s) correctly show the decomposition of the number into a group of 10 in one frame and the remaining cubes in a second frame?

- Did the student(s) have difficulty with any particular number?

- What procedure did the student(s) use to show the decomposition? Did they count out 10 cubes first and then place them in one frame? Did they fill a ten-frame directly with 10 cubes?

# 26: Solve the Problem

## (i) Number of Students

Individuals or partner pairs

## (/) Materials

For each student or pair:

• Problem-Solving Cards (page 143)

For each student:

• Ten-frame or Ten Frames Template (page 110)

• 20 Unifix Cubes (or other markers), 10 of one color and 10 of a different color

## (◆) Overview

In this activity, students respond to oral or written problems involving Unifix Cubes, some of which have more than one solution.

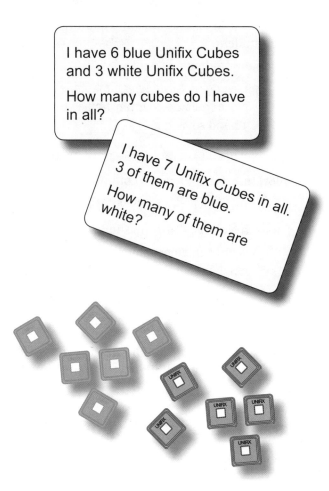

I have 6 blue Unifix Cubes and 3 white Unifix Cubes.

How many cubes do I have in all?

I have 7 Unifix Cubes in all. 3 of them are blue. How many of them are white?

## Common Core State Standards

### Content Standards:

**Grade Level:** 1

**Domain:** Operations and Algebraic Thinking (1.OA)

**Represent and solve problems involving addition and subtraction.**

1. Use addition and subtraction within 20 to solve word problems involving situations of adding to, taking from, putting together, taking apart, and comparing, with unknowns in all positions, e.g., by using objects, drawings, and equations with a symbol for the unknown number to represent the problem.

### Practice Standards:

1. **Make sense of problems and persevere in solving them.**

   Students must explain to themselves and to their classmates what the information means for each problem. In certain situations, problems can have more than one solution.

2. **Reason abstractly and quantitatively.**

   Students must make sense of the quantities involved on each problem card, manipulating objects in a quantitative manner to solve the problems.

# Presenting the Activity

1. Make copies of the Problem-Solving Cards on card stock and cut them apart.

2. If the blank Problem-Solving Cards are used, write appropriate numbers on the blank lines.

3. Make copies of the Ten-Frames Template, if using.

4. Distribute 20 Unifix Cubes to each student. Note that the cards use blue and white cubes only.

5. Depending upon a student's ability to read, distribute the Problem-Solving Cards or read the cards to the students.

6. Say to the student(s):

   (( Use your ten-frame and the Unifix Cubes to solve the problem on the card.

7. You may need to demonstrate the activity with one card.

8. Allow time for students to complete the task.

9. Repeat the activity for several Problem-Solving Cards.

10. For each card selected, say to the student(s):

    (( Is there one answer or more than one answer to this problem?

# Assessing Student Responses

The following questions will help you assess your students' responses to the activity:

- Did the student(s) correctly model the solution(s) to each problem situation?

- If the problem had more than one correct answer, did the student(s): (a) model each solution with the cubes, (b) just state that there was more than one answer to the problem, or (c) state the answers without showing them with the cubes?

- If the student(s) answered a problem incorrectly, did they incorrectly solve a similar problem?

- For incorrect solutions, what approach did the student(s) use to solve the problem?

- Did the student(s) have difficulty reading the Problem-Solving Cards?

# 27: Where Are You?

## (i) Number of Students

Entire class in pairs

## (/) Materials

For each pair of students:

• Ten-Frame Cards 1–10, 4 sets (page 114)

## (◆) Overview

In this activity, pairs of students find the sum of their two Ten-Frame Cards. If the sum is not 20, they find another pair who has the missing addend that will produce a sum of 20.

## Common Core State Standards

### Content Standards:

**Grade Level:** 1

**Domain:** Operations and Algebraic Thinking (1.OA)

**Represent and solve problems involving addition and subtraction.**

1. Use addition and subtraction within 20 to solve word problems involving situations of adding to, taking from, putting together, taking apart, and comparing, with unknowns in all positions, e.g., by using objects, drawings, and equations with a symbol for the unknown number to represent the problem.

### Practice Standards:

1. **Make sense of problems and persevere in solving them.**

   Students must explain to themselves and to their classmates what the information means for each problem. In certain situations, problems can have more than one solution.

2. **Reason abstractly and quantitatively.**

   Students must make sense of the quantities involved on each card, manipulating objects in a quantitative manner to solve the problems.

# ⬛ Presenting the Activity

1.  Make 4 copies of the Ten-Frame Cards on card stock and cut them apart.

2.  Group students into pairs.

3.  Distribute a Ten-Frame Card to each student.

4.  Say to the student(s):

    > 66 With your partner, find the sum of the two numbers represented on your ten-frames.
    >
    > Then write a number sentence showing the sum. For example, if one of you has 3 and the other has 5, write "3 + 5 = 8."
    >
    > When you finish, write a subtraction number sentence to show what you need to have a sum of 20. (20 − 8 = 12.)
    >
    > You need to find a pair whose Ten-Frame Cards sum to 12. When you do, go stand together with the other pair.

5.  The first two pairs that make a sum of 20 win the game.

6.  Allow time for students to complete the game.

7.  At the completion of the game, collect the cards, redistribute them to the pairs, and play a second game.

# ◎ Assessing Student Responses

The following questions will help you assess your students' responses to the activity:

*   Did the pairs of students correctly find the sum of the two numbers represented on the ten-frames?

*   Did the pairs of students correctly write the two number sentences?

*   If the student(s) gave an incorrect sum, is there an observable error pattern?

*   Were the pairs of students able to find another pair to make a sum of 20?

# 28: Who Am I?

## (i) Number of Students

Partner pairs

## (/) Materials

For each pair of students:

- Ten-Frame Cards 1–20 (pages 114–115)
- "Who Am I?" Cards (pages 145–147)

## (◆) Overview

In this activity, students respond to oral or written problems involving numbers from 1 to 20, some of which have more than one solution.

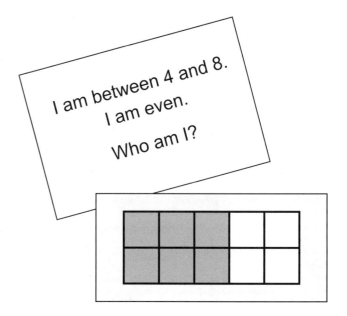

I am between 4 and 8.
I am even.
Who am I?

---

## Common Core State Standards

### Content Standards:

**Grade Level:** 1

**Domain:** Operations and Algebraic Thinking (1.OA)

**Represent and solve problems involving addition and subtraction.**

1. Use addition and subtraction within 20 to solve word problems involving situations of adding to, taking from, putting together, taking apart, and comparing, with unknowns in all positions, e.g., by using objects, drawings, and equations with a symbol for the unknown number to represent the problem.

**Domain:** Number and Operations in Base Ten (1.NBT)

**Understand place value.**

2. Understand that the two digits of a two-digit number represent amounts of tens and ones. Understand the following as special cases:

a. 10 can be thought of as a bundle of ten ones—called a "ten."

b. The numbers from 11 to 19 are composed of a ten and one, two, three, four, five, six, seven, eight, or nine ones.

### Practice Standards:

1. **Make sense of problems and persevere in solving them.**

   Students must explain to themselves and to their classmates what the information means for each problem. In certain situations, problems can have more than one solution.

2. **Reason abstractly and quantitatively.**

   Students must make sense of mathematical vocabulary for the quantities involved on each problem card.

---

# ⬛ Presenting the Activity

1.  Make copies of the Ten-Frame Cards and the "Who Am I?" Cards on card stock and cut them apart.

2.  Distribute the Ten-Frame Cards and the "Who Am I?" Cards to each pair of students.

3.  Depending upon the students' ability to read, you may need to read the cards to students.

4.  Say to the students:

    > 66 Place the Ten-Frame Cards from 1 to 20 in front of both of you.
    >
    > One of you starts by selecting a "Who Am I?" Card and reading the problem.
    >
    > Your partner finds the Ten-Frame Card or cards that answers the question "Who am I?"
    >
    > Remember, some cards will have more than one number for an answer. Be sure to find all of the numbers.

5.  You may need to demonstrate the activity with one card.

6.  Allow time for students to complete the task.

7.  Repeat the activity until all "Who Am I?" Cards have been used.

8.  For each card selected, say to student(s):

    > Is there one answer or more than one answer to this problem?
    >
    > If there is more than one number, how did you know?

# ⦿ Assessing Student Responses

The following questions will help you assess your students' responses to the activity:

*   Did the student(s) correctly find the cards for each problem situation?

*   If the problem had more than one correct answer, how did the student(s) determine the multiple answers?

*   If the student(s) did not find all solutions to a problem, did you observe or hear any strategies they might have used?

*   Did the student(s) have difficulty reading the "Who Am I?" Cards?

*   Did the student(s) have difficulty with any particular problem format?

# 29: I Know That Problem

## (i) Number of Students

Entire class in partner pairs

## (/) Materials

For each student:

• 2 ten-frames or Ten-Frames Template (page 110)

For each pair of students:

• 20 Unifix Cubes

• Individual student whiteboard and marker

For the teacher:

• Word Problem Cards (page 148)

## (◆) Overview

In this activity, students solve word problems involving addition and subtraction of whole numbers. The word problems are read by the teacher or may be read by students, if able.

Matt had 14 marbles. Kent gave him 4 more marbles. How many marbles does he have now?

I have 11 shirts. Six of my shirts are blue. How many shirts are not blue?

## Common Core State Standards

### Content Standards:

**Grade Level:** 1

**Domain:** Operations and Algebraic Thinking (1.OA)

**Represent and solve problems involving addition and subtraction.**

1. Use addition and subtraction within 20 to solve word problems involving situations of adding to, taking from, putting together, taking apart, and comparing, with unknowns in all positions, e.g., by using objects, drawings, and equations with a symbol for the unknown number to represent the problem.

### Practice Standards:

1. **Make sense of problems and persevere in solving them.**
   Students must explain to themselves and to their classmates what the information means for each problem. In certain situations, problems can have more than one solution.

2. **Reason abstractly and quantitatively.**
   Students must make sense of mathematical vocabulary for the quantities involved on each problem card.

3. **Construct viable arguments and critique the reasoning of others.**
   Students justify their conclusions and communicate them to others.

4. **Model with mathematics.**
   Students use Unifix Cubes and ten-frames to model and solve word problems.

# ⬛ Presenting the Activity

1. Make one copy of the Word Problem Cards and cut the cards apart.

2. Group the students into partner pairs.

3. Distribute Unifix Cubes and ten-frames to each pair of students.

4. Say to the students:

   > **❝** I will select and read one of the Word Problem Cards out loud to the class.
   >
   > For example, Mike checked out 8 books from the library. He read 3 books today. How many more books does he need to read before returning the books to the library?
   >
   > Partner 1 will solve the problem using Unifix Cubes and ten-frames.
   >
   > Partner 1 will set up the problem by placing 8 Unifix Cubes on the ten-frame, and then remove 3 cubes to model the answer, 5.
   >
   > Partner 1, explain your thinking as you solve the problem.
   >
   > Partner 2, listen to how your partner is solving the problem. Then, using your whiteboard, write a number sentence to represent the problem, such as $8 - 3 = 5$.
   >
   > Then, the two partners trade roles.
   >
   > I will select another problem card to read to the class.
   >
   > Partner 2 will model the solution using Unifix Cubes and ten-frames, then share the answer with Partner 1, who will create the number sentence.

5. As time allows, continue reading problems for students to solve.

# ◎ Assessing Student Responses

The following questions will help you assess your students' responses to the activity.

- Did the student(s) correctly model each problem with the Unifix Cubes and ten-frames?

- Did the student(s) use the appropriate terminology, such as *added to, joined, subtracted, equals,* and so on?

- Did the student(s) state the correct solution for each word problem?

- Did the student(s) create correct equations?

- If the student gave an incorrect answer to a word problem after modeling it correctly, was any pattern evident?

# 30: Sum to 20

## ⓘ Number of Students

2–3

## ⊘ Materials

For each group:

• Ten-Frame Cards 1–20, 2 sets (pages 114–115)

• Scrap paper

## ◈ Overview

The game, like "Go Fish," involves students asking for Ten-Frame Cards from other players to make the sum of 20 using two or three cards.

## Common Core State Standards

### Content Standards:

**Grade Level:** 1

**Domain:** Operations and Algebraic Thinking (1.OA)

**Represent and solve problems involving addition and subtraction.**

2. Solve word problems that call for addition of three whole numbers whose sum is less than or equal to 20, e.g., by using objects, drawings, and equations with a symbol for the unknown number to represent the problem.

**Add and subtract within 20.**

6. Add and subtract within 20, demonstrating fluency for addition and subtraction within 10.

### Practice Standards:

2. **Reason abstractly and quantitatively.**

   Students have been making 10 using various strategies, such as counting on. They incorporate these strategies in working with more than two addends.

7. **Look for and make use of structure.**

   Activities that focus on subitization have been used extensively in Kindergarten. Similar observations work with sums to 20.

# ⊞ Presenting the Activity

1. Distribute a deck of Ten-Frame Cards to each group of players

2. Say to the students:

   ❝ This is a card game like "Go Fish." One of you starts by dealing three cards to each player. Then place the remaining cards facedown on the playing area.

   Look at your cards. You want the numbers represented on the ten-frames to add up to 20.

   If you have two or three cards in your hand that add up to 20, or if you have the 20 Ten-Frame Card, lay down those cards on your turn.

   On scrap paper, write an addition number sentence showing the sum you have.

   If none of your cards add up to 20, figure out what Ten-Frame Card you need to make 20. Write a subtraction number sentence to show what you need to make 20. Then, on your turn, ask the player on your left for that particular Ten-Frame Card.

   If the player has that card, he or she gives it to you. You can then lay down your cards that sum to 20. If the player does not have the card you need, he or she will say "Go Fish" and you will need to draw a Ten-Frame Card from the deck.

   Then the next player will ask for a card.

   Every time you lay down all or some of your cards, draw again so that you always have three cards in your hand.

3. The game is over when all of the cards have been drawn. The player who has laid down the most cards is the winner.

4. You may need to provide an example for students, such as the following:

   ❝ I have a Ten-Frame Card representing 2, another one representing 5, and another representing 7. So, $2 + 5 + 7 = 14$. What Ten-Frame Card should I ask for on my turn?

   I could ask for 6, so I could lay down all of my cards.

   I could ask for 13, since $2 + 5 + 13 = 20$.

   I could ask for 11, since $2 + 7 + 11 = 20$.

   I could ask for 8, since $5 + 7 + 8 = 20$.

5. Allow time for students to finish the game.

# ⊘ Assessing Student Responses

- The following questions will help you assess your students' responses to the activities:

- Did the student(s) correctly find the sum of numbers represented on the Ten-Frame Cards?

- Did the student(s) write the correct addition number sentence for each turn?

- Did the student(s) write the correct subtraction number sentence for each turn?

- Did the student(s) use any noticeable fact strategies in finding the sums or differences?

# 31: Train Trip

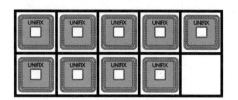

## ⓘ Number of Students

Entire class with partner pairs

## ⊘ Materials

For each student:
- 2 ten-frames or Ten-Frames Template (page 110)

For each pair of students:
- 30 Unifix Cubes
- Individual student whiteboard and marker

For the teacher:
- "Train Trip" Word Problem Cards (page 149)

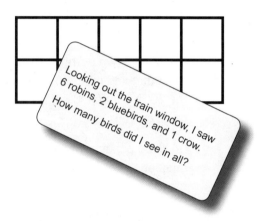

Looking out the train window, I saw 6 robins, 2 bluebirds, and 1 crow. How many birds did I see in all?

## ◈ Overview

In this activity, students solve word problems about traveling on a train that involve the addition of three whole numbers. The word problems are read by the teacher or may be read by the students, if able.

## Common Core State Standards

### Content Standards:

**Grade Level:** 1

**Domain:** Operations and Algebraic Thinking (1.OA)

**Represent and solve problems involving addition and subtraction.**

2. Solve word problems that call for addition of three whole numbers whose sum is less than or equal to 20, e.g., by using objects, drawings, and equations with a symbol for the unknown number to represent the problem.

### Practice Standards:

1. **Make sense of problems and persevere in solving them.**

   Students must explain to themselves and to their classmates what the information means for each problem.

2. **Reason abstractly and quantitatively.**

   Students must make sense of the quantities involved on each problem card, manipulating objects in a quantitative manner to solve the problems.

4. **Model with mathematics.**

   Students are using Unifix Cubes and ten-frames to model addition word problems of three whole numbers.

# Presenting the Activity

1. Reproduce the "Train Trip" Word Problem Cards and cut the cards apart.

2. Reproduce the Ten-Frames Templates, if using, per partner pair.

3. Group the students into partner pairs.

4. Distribute the ten-frames or a copy of the Ten-Frames Template to each partner pair.

5. Distribute 20 Unifix Cubes per partner pair.

6. Distribute 5 additional Unifix Cubes to each student.

7. The teacher or leader begins the activity by reading a Word Problem Card.

8. Say to the students:

   " Student 1 will begin by using Unifix Cubes on the ten-frames to solve the problem. Here is an example:

   *Lashonda takes 4 books to read on her train trip. Her brother Franco takes 5 books with him and her other brother Mario takes 6 books. How many books did the children take to read on the trip?*

9. Demonstrate how to use the cubes to solve the problem, or have Student 1 fill the ten-frames.

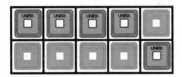

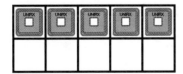

10. Say to Student 1:

   " By placing the cubes on the ten-frame, how many books did the family take on the trip?

   If you solve a problem correctly on your turn, you will be given a Unifix cube to begin creating a Unifix train.

With each problem you solve correctly, your Unifix train will grow one cube at a time.

11. Give Student 2 a word problem to solve, and repeat the process.

12. The activity concludes when you have completed 3–5 rounds.

# Assessing Student Responses

- The following questions will help you assess your students' responses to the activity:

- Did the student(s) correctly model each addition problem with the cubes and ten-frames?

- Did the student(s) use the appropriate terminology such as *added to, joined,* or *equals?*

- Did the student(s) state the correct sum for each word problem?

- Did the student(s) use any noticeable fact strategies in finding the sums?

- If a student answered several word problems incorrectly after showing the model correctly, was any pattern evident?

# 32: What's on My Head?

## ⓘ Number of Students

Small group (3–4 students)

## ⊘ Materials

- Ten-Frame Cards 1–10, 3 sets (page 114)

## ◈ Overview

In this activity, one student finds the sum of numbers represented on ten-frames. Two or three other students determine what their "hidden" numbers are.

## Common Core State Standards

### Content Standards:

**Grade Level:** 1

**Domain:** Operations and Algebraic Thinking (1.OA)

**Understand and apply properties of operations and the relationship between addition and subtraction.**

3. Apply properties of operations as strategies to add and subtract.

**Add and subtract within 20.**

5. Relate counting to addition and subtraction.

6. Add and subtract within 20, demonstrating fluency for addition and subtraction within 10.

### Practice Standards:

1. **Make sense of problems and persevere in solving them.**

   Students must explain to themselves and to their classmates what the information means for each group of hidden ten-frames.

2. **Reason abstractly and quantitatively.**

   Students must make sense of the quantities involved on each Ten-Frame Card they observe.

# 🖥 Presenting the Activity

1.  Make 3 copies of the Ten-Frame Cards on card stock and cut them apart.

2.  Form students into groups of 3 (or 4, depending on facility with addition to 30).

3.  Distribute a set of Ten-Frame cards to each group.

4.  Say to the students:

    > 💬 The dealer starts by dealing one card facedown to the other two (three) players.
    >
    > When you say "Go!" the other players hold their cards on their forehead without looking at them. (Illustrate with a card.)
    >
    > The dealer finds the sum of numbers on the cards the other players are holding on their foreheads. The dealer tells the other players the sum.
    >
    > Since each player can see the other players' numbers, they can now figure out what number is on their own head.
    >
    > After the players tell what number they think is on their own forehead, let them check by looking at their cards.

5.  Allow time for students to finish a game.

6.  When the game is over, play a second game with a different student acting as dealer (finding the sum).

7.  Allow time for students to play three or more games, so every student has a chance to find the sum. If you are using all 30 Ten-Frame Cards, each player in a group of three could have five turns finding the sum.

# ✅ Assessing Student Responses

The following questions will help you assess your students' responses to the activity:

*   Did the student(s) correctly find the sum of the two numbers represented on the ten-frames?

*   Did each student correctly identify the number on his or her head?

*   If a student gave an incorrect sum, is there an observable error pattern?

# 33: Addition Action

## ⓘ Number of Students

Individual or pairs

## ⊘ Materials

For each student:

• "Addition Action" Activity Sheet (page 153)

For each pair of students:

• Addition Fact Cards (page 150–152)
• 20 Unifix Cubes, 10 each of 2 different colors

## ◈ Overview

The activity involves students drawing a card showing two addends, placing cubes on ten-frames, and then stating the sum.

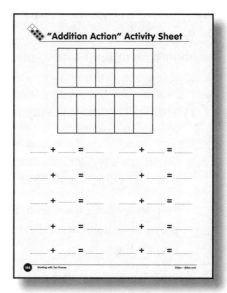

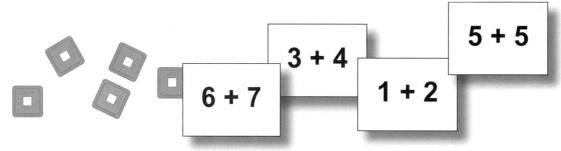

---

## Common Core State Standards

### Content Standards:

**Grade Level:** 1

**Domain:** Operations and Algebraic Thinking (1.OA)

**Understand and apply properties of operations and the relationship between addition and subtraction.**

**3.** Apply properties of operations as strategies to add and subtract.

**Add and subtract within 20.**

**6.** Add and subtract within 20, demonstrating fluency for addition and subtraction within 10.

### Practice Standards:

**7. Look for and make use of structure.**

The structure comes in the form of properties of addition. For this particular activity, the commutative property is the important piece for students to understand.

**8. Look for and express regularity in repeated reasoning.**

Students have explored ideas about making 10 in kindergarten. A similar idea now comes to the forefront in making 20—for example, 18 + 2, 16 + 4, or 19 + 1.

---

# ◉ Presenting the Activity

1. Make copies of the Addition Fact Cards on card stock and cut them apart. Note that all facts are not included.

2. Distribute Unifix Cubes and a set of Addition Fact Cards to each pair.

3. Distribute an "Addition Action" Activity Sheet to each student.

4. Say to the student(s):

   > 💬 One of you starts by drawing an Addition Fact Card. Show the two addends on your ten-frames with your cubes. Use a different color for each addend. When you finish placing cubes on the frames, state the sum to your partner and write the number sentence on your paper.

5. You may need to demonstrate the activity with one card.

6. Allow time for students to complete the task.

7. Have students repeat the activity for at least 10 Addition Fact Cards each.

# ◉ Assessing Student Responses

The following questions will help you assess your students' responses to the activities:

- Did the student(s) correctly model each addition problem with the cubes?

- Did the student(s) state the correct sum for each problem?

- Did the student(s) use any noticeable fact strategies in finding the sums?

- If a student answered incorrectly to several problems after showing the model correctly, was any pattern evident?

# 34: Subtraction Action

## (i) Number of Students

Individual or pairs

## (∕) Materials

For each student:

• "Subtraction Action" Activity Sheet (page 157)

For each pair of students:

• Subtraction Fact Cards (pages 154–156)
• 20 Unifix Cubes of one color

## (◈) Overview

The activity involves students drawing a card showing a subtraction problem (known sum and known addend), placing cubes on ten-frames, removing cubes, and then stating the difference.

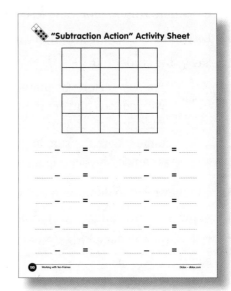

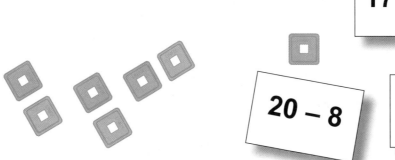

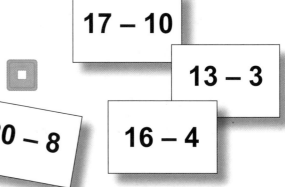

---

## Common Core State Standards

### Content Standards:

**Grade Level:** 1

**Domain:** Operations and Algebraic Thinking (1.OA)

**Understand and apply properties of operations and the relationship between addition and subtraction.**

3. Apply properties of operations as strategies to add and subtract.

**Add and subtract within 20.**

6. Add and subtract within 20, demonstrating fluency for addition and subtraction within 10.

### Practice Standards:

7. **Look for and make use of structure.**

   Students understand that subtraction is the inverse operation of addition. For example, if $6 + 7 = 13$, then $13 - 6 = 7$ and $13 - 7 = 6$.

# ⬛ Presenting Activity

1. Make copies of the Subtraction Fact Cards on card stock and cut them apart. Note that all facts are not included.

2. Distribute Unifix Cubes and a set of Subtraction Fact Cards to each pair.

3. Distribute a "Subtraction Action" Activity Sheet to each student.

4. Say to the student(s):

   > 66 One of you starts by drawing a Subtraction Fact Card. Use cubes of one color to show the first number. When you finish placing cubes on the frames, remove the number of cubes represented by the second number on the card. State the difference to your partner and write the number sentence on your paper.

5. You may need to demonstrate the activity with one card.

6. Allow time for students to complete the task.

7. Have students repeat the activity for at least 10 Subtraction Fact Cards each.

# ⊘ Assessing Student Responses

The following questions will help you assess your students' responses to the activity:

- Did the student(s) correctly model each subtraction problem with the cubes?

- Did the student(s) state the correct difference for each problem?

- Did the student(s) use any noticeable fact strategies to find the differences?

- If the student answered several problems incorrectly after showing the model correctly, was any pattern evident?

# 35: Make My Target Number

## ⓘ Number of Students

Pairs

## ✎ Materials

For each student:
- "Make My Target Number" Activity Sheet (page 158)
- 20 Unifix Cubes

For each pair of students:
- Number Cards 11–20 (pages 118–119)
- Six-sided number cube or 1–6 Spinner (page 159)

## ◈ Overview

The activity involves students tossing a number cube, placing Unifix Cubes on ten-frames, and writing the corresponding number sentence until reaching a specified number.

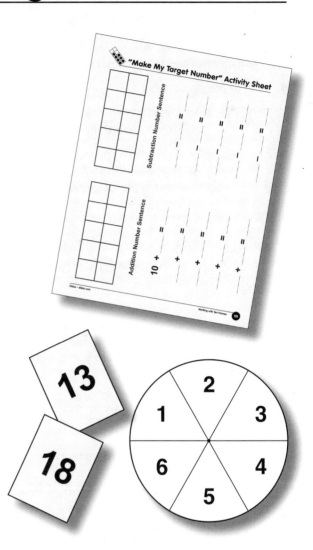

## Common Core State Standards

### Content Standards:

**Grade Level:** 1

**Domain:** Operations and Algebraic Thinking (1.OA)
**Add and subtract within 20.**

6. Add and subtract within 20, demonstrating fluency for addition and subtraction within 10.

### Practice Standards:

2. **Reason abstractly and quantitatively.**

   Students have been making 10 using various strategies, such as counting on. Similar strategies work for finding a sum up to 20.

4. **Model with mathematics.**

   Students model two addends with cubes and then write a corresponding number sentence representing the sum.

# Presenting the Activity

1. Distribute Unifix Cubes and a "Make My Target Number" Activity Sheet to each student.

2. Distribute a 1–6 number cube or 1–6 spinner sheet to each pair.

3. Say to the student(s):

   > To start the game, each one of you draws a Number Card. Whoever has the greater number goes first. This is the target number you need to make on your ten-frames.

4. Now, fill in one of the ten-frames with 10 Unifix Cubes.

5. Allow time for students to complete the task.

6. Say to the student(s):

   > On your turn, toss the number cube and pick up the corresponding number of cubes. Place them on your ten-frames. The object of the games is to reach your target number before your opponent. For each turn, I want you to write two number sentences. The first is an addition number sentence to show the sum. When you start, the first number sentence will be "10 plus your number equals a new number."
   >
   > The second number sentence will be a subtraction number sentence to show the number of cubes you need to reach your target number. If your target number is 16 and you toss 2, then your first equation will be $10 + 2 = 12$ and your second equation will be $16 - 12 = 4$.
   >
   > You have to get your target number exactly to win. So, if you toss a number that will give you more than your target number, you lose your turn. For example, if you have 12 cubes in your frames and toss a 5, you would lose your turn.

## Assessing Student Responses

The following questions will help you assess your students' responses to the activity:

- Did the student(s) correctly model each addition problem with the cubes?

- Did the student(s) write the correct addition number sentence for each toss?

- Did the student(s) write the correct subtraction number sentence for each toss?

- Did the student(s) use any noticeable fact strategies in finding the differences?

- If the student answered incorrectly to several problems after showing the model correctly, was any pattern evident?

# 36: Diffy

## ⓘ Number of Students

Pairs

## ⊘ Materials

For each pair of students:

- Ten-Frame Cards 1–20, 3 sets (pages 114–115)
- 60 Unifix Cubes

## ◈ Overview

In this activity, students draw two ten-frame cards showing representations of numbers between 1 and 20. They find the difference between the two numbers.

## Common Core State Standards

### Content Standards:

**Grade Level:** 1

**Domain:** Operations and Algebraic Thinking (1.OA)

**Add and subtract within 20.**

6. Add and subtract within 20, demonstrating fluency for addition and subtraction within 10.

### Practice Standards:

6. **Attend to precision.**

Students learn that addition and subtraction are inverse operations. Their early focus is on differences to 10. For this particular game, students accurately calculate differences to 20.

# ⬚ Presenting the Activity

1. Make copies of the Ten-Frame Cards on card stock and cut them apart. Form decks using 3 sets of the cards.

2. Distribute 60 Unifix Cubes to each pair.

3. Distribute a deck of Ten-Frame Cards to each pair.

4. Say to the student(s):

   > Partner 1 starts by drawing two Ten-Frame Cards and placing them on the table so both of you can see the cards.
   >
   > Partner 1, write a number sentence subtracting the smaller number from the larger number. When you find the difference, take that many cubes from the pile.
   >
   > Place the two cards in a separate pile.
   >
   > Now, Partner 2 draws two cards and subtracts.

5. You may need to demonstrate the activity with two cards.

6. Say to the students:

   > Keep playing until all the cards have been paired.
   >
   > The winner is the player with more cubes or counters.

7. Allow time for students to complete the task.

# ⊘ Assessing Student Responses

The following questions will help you assess your students' responses to the activity:

- Did the student(s) accurately find the difference of the two numbers?

- Did the student(s) write the correct number sentences?

- Did the student(s) use any noticeable strategies in finding the differences?

- If a student answered incorrectly to several problems after drawing the cards, was any pattern evident?

# 37: 20 Match

## ⓘ Number of Students

Pairs

## ⊘ Materials

For each pair of students:

- Number Cards 1–20 (pages 117–119)
- Ten-Frame Cards 1–10, 2 sets (pages 114–115)

## ◈ Overview

In this game students draw two Ten-Frame Cards, find the sum, and select the Number Card that represents the sum.

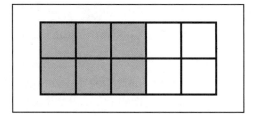

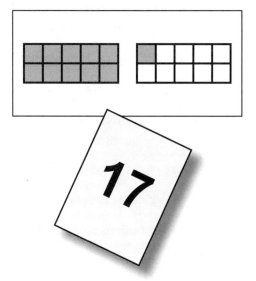

---

## Common Core State Standards

### Content Standards:

**Grade Level:** 1

**Domain:** Operations and Algebraic Thinking (1.OA)

**Add and subtract within 20.**

6. Add and subtract within 20, demonstrating fluency for addition and subtraction within 10.

### Practice Standards:

1. **Make sense of problems and persevere in solving them.**

   Students analyze multiple ten-frame patterns based on earlier work with a single ten-frame to find sums to 20.

2. **Reason abstractly and quantitatively.**

   Students have been making 10 using various strategies, such as counting on. Similar strategies work for finding a sum to 20.

---

# ⬛ Presenting the Activity

1. Distribute 2 sets of Ten-Frame Cards and a set of Number Cards to each pair.

2. Say to the student(s):

   > 66 To determine who starts the game, each one of you draws a Number Card. Whoever has the greater number goes first.
   >
   > Now, place the Number Cards face up in order from 1 to 20.
   >
   > Place the Ten-Frame Cards facedown in a pile.
   >
   > On your turn, draw two Ten-Frame Cards, find the sum, and then pick up the Number Card with the corresponding sum.
   >
   > If you draw two Ten-Frame Cards and the Number Card has already been taken for that sum, you lose your turn.
   >
   > The player who has more Number Cards after all the Ten-Frame Cards have been drawn is the winner.

3. Allow time for students to complete the game.

# ⊙ Assessing Student Responses

The following questions will help you assess your students' responses to the activity:

- Did the student(s) accurately find the sum of the two ten-frame numbers?

- Did the student(s) use any noticeable fact strategies in finding the sums?

- Did the student(s) count individual squares to find the sums?

# 38: First to 20

## ⓘ Number of Students

Pairs

## ⊘ Materials

For each student:
- "First to 20" Activity Sheet (page 160)
- 20 Unifix Cubes

For each pair of students:
- Six-sided number cube or 1–6 Spinner (page 159)

## ◈ Overview

In this activity students toss a number cube or spin a spinner, place Unifix Cubes on ten-frames, and write the corresponding number sentences until they have exactly 20 Unifix Cubes in their ten-frames.

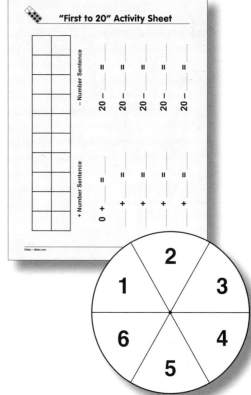

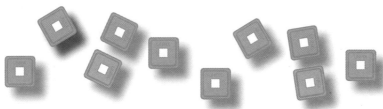

## Common Core State Standards

### Content Standards:

**Grade Level:** 1

**Domain:** Operations and Algebraic Thinking (1.OA)

**Add and subtract within 20.**

6. Add and subtract within 20, demonstrating fluency for addition and subtraction within 10.

### Practice Standards:

2. **Reason abstractly and quantitatively.**

   Students have been making 10 using various strategies, such as counting on. Similar strategies work for finding a sum to 20.

4. **Model with mathematics.**

   Students model two addends with cubes and then write a corresponding number sentence representing the sum.

# ⊡ Presenting the Activity

1. Distribute Unifix Cubes and an activity sheet to each student.

2. Distribute a number cube to each pair.

3. Say to the students:

   **❝** To determine who starts the game, each of you toss the number cube. Whoever has the greater number goes first.

4. Allow time for students to complete the task.

5. Say to the students:

   **❝** On your turn, toss the number cube and pick up the corresponding number of cubes. Place them on your ten-frames. The object of the game is to completely fill your frames with 20 cubes.

   For each turn, I want you to write two number sentences. The first is an addition number sentence to show the sum. When you start, the first number sentence will be "0 plus the number you tossed equals your number."

   The second number sentence will be a subtraction number sentence to show the number of cubes you need to reach 20. It will always be 20 minus the number of cubes you have on your ten-frames (for example, $20 - 14 = 6$).

   You have to have exactly 20 cubes on your frames to win. So, if you toss a number that will give you more than 20, you lose your turn. For example, if you have 17 cubes on your frames and you toss a 5, you will lose your turn.

# ⊘ Assessing Student Responses

The following questions will help you assess your students' responses to the activity:

- Did the student(s) correctly model each addition problem with the cubes?

- Did the student(s) write the correct addition number sentence for each toss?

- Did the student(s) write the correct subtraction number sentence for each toss?

- Did the student(s) use any noticeable fact strategies in finding the differences?

- If a student answered incorrectly to several problems after showing the model correctly, was any pattern evident?

# 39: First to Zero

## (i) Number of Students

Pairs

## (/) Materials

For each student:
- "First to Zero" Activity Sheet (page 161)
- 20 Unifix Cubes

For each pair of students:
- Six-sided number cube or 1–6 Spinner (page 159)

## (◆) Overview

In this activity students fill the ten-frames with 20 Unifix Cubes, toss a 1–6 number cube, remove the corresponding number of cubes from the ten-frames, and write the corresponding subtraction number sentences until they have exactly zero Unifix Cubes in their ten-frames.

---

## Common Core State Standards

### Content Standards:

**Grade Level:** 1

**Domain:** Operations and Algebraic Thinking (1.OA)

**Add and subtract within 20.**

6. Add and subtract within 20, demonstrating fluency for addition and subtraction within 10.

### Practice Standards:

2. **Reason abstractly and quantitatively.**

    Students have learned that addition and subtraction are inverse operations. They used this reasoning with sums and differences to 10, and now extend the reasoning.

4. **Model with mathematics.**

    Students model a known sum (minuend) and known addend (subtrahend) with cubes and then write a corresponding number sentence representing the difference.

# ▣ Presenting the Activity

1. Distribute Unifix Cubes and an activity sheet to each student.

2. Distribute a number cube to each pair.

3. Say to the student(s):

   **❝** Each of you, toss the number cube. Whoever has the greater number goes first.

   Now, each of you fill your ten-frames with the 20 Unifix Cubes.

4. Allow time for students to complete the task.

5. Say to the students:

   **❝** On your turn, toss the number cube and remove the corresponding number of cubes from your ten-frames. The object of the game is to remove all 20 cubes from your ten-frames.

   For each turn, I want you to write a subtraction number sentence. The first subtraction number sentence you write will be "20 minus your number equals the difference."

   After you start, the number sentence will be a subtraction number sentence to show the number of cubes you have remaining on your frames. For example, if you have 15 cubes on your frames and toss a 4, then your subtraction number sentence will be $15 - 4 = 11$.

   You have to have exactly 0 cubes in your frames to win. So, if you toss a number that will not give you 0, you lose your turn. For example, if you have 4 cubes in your frames and toss a 5, you will lose your turn.

# ◉ Assessing Student Responses

The following questions will help you assess your students' responses to the activity:

- Did the student(s) correctly model each subtraction problem with the cubes?

- Did the student(s) write the correct subtraction number sentence for each toss?

- Did the student(s) use any noticeable fact strategies in finding the differences?

- If a student answered several problems incorrectly after showing the model correctly, was any pattern evident?

# 40: Difference War

## (i) Number of Students

Pairs

## (/) Materials

For each pair of students:

• Ten-Frame Cards 1–20 (pages 114–115)

For each student:

• 60 Unifix Cubes or other counters

## (◈) Overview

In this activity two students each draw a Ten-Frame Card showing a representation of a number between 1 and 20. The student with the greater number wins Unifix Cubes or counters corresponding to the difference between the two numbers.

## Common Core State Standards

### Content Standards:

**Grade Level:** K

**Domain:** Counting and Cardinality (K.CC)

**Compare numbers.**

6. Identify whether the number of objects in one group is greater than, less than, or equal to the number of objects in another group, e.g., by using matching and counting strategies.

**Grade Level:** 1

**Domain:** Operations and Algebraic Thinking (1.OA)

**Add and subtract within 20.**

6. Add and subtract within 20, demonstrating fluency for addition and subtraction within 10.

### Practice Standards:

7. **Look for and make use of structure.**

   Students have found differences to 10. They discern earlier patterns as they now subtract within 20, such as $7 - 2 = 5$ and $17 - 2 = 15$.

# ⬚ Presenting the Activity

1. Make copies of the Ten-Frame Cards on card stock and cut them apart.

2. Distribute a deck of Ten-Frame Cards to each student.

3. Distribute 60 Unifix Cubes or other counters to each pair.

4. Say to the students:

   **❝** Place your set of Ten-Frame Cards facedown in front of you.

   Now, each of you turn over a card.

   Whoever has the greater number wins the round.

   The winner subtracts the smaller number from the larger number, and takes that many cubes from the pile.

5. You may need to demonstrate the activity with two cards.

6. Say to the student(s):

   **❝** Keep playing until all the cards have been played.

   The winner is the player with more counters.

   If you both turn over the same number on a round, turn over another card.

7. Allow time for students to complete the task.

# ⊘ Assessing Student Responses

The following questions will help you assess your students' responses to the activity:

- Did the student(s) compare the two numbers correctly?

- Did the student(s) accurately find the difference between the two numbers?

- Did the student(s) use any noticeable strategies in finding the differences?

# 41: Missing Markers

## ⓘ Number of Students

Pairs

## ✐ Materials

For each student:

- 10 Unifix Cubes

For each pair of students:

- Number Cards 0–9, 2 sets (pages 117, 120)
- Ten-Frame Spinner (page 162)

## ◈ Overview

In this activity students find a missing addend to make a group of 10.

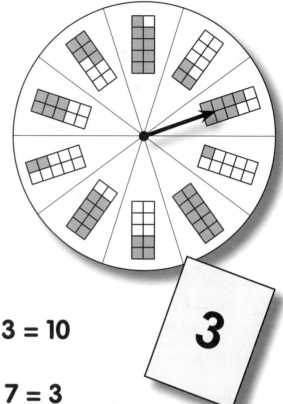

$$7 + 3 = 10$$

$$10 - 7 = 3$$

**3**

## Common Core State Standards

**Content Standards:**

**Grade Level:** 1

**Domain:** Operations and Algebraic Thinking (1.OA)

**Add and subtract within 20.**

6. Add and subtract within 20, demonstrating fluency for addition and subtraction within 10.

**Practice Standards:**

2. **Reason abstractly and quantitatively.**

   Students find missing addends based on representations of known addends on ten-frames.

6. **Attend to precision.**

   Students communicate their understanding of addition by writing a number sentence corresponding to the ten-frames number and the missing addend.

# ⊡ Presenting the Activity

1. Distribute two sets of number cards and a spinner to each pair of students.

2. Distribute 10 Unifix Cubes to each student.

3. Say to the student(s):

   ❝ The object of the game is to make 10 by finding a missing addend.

   Shuffle the Number Cards and place them facedown between you. Turn over 6 cards and place them face up in a row.

   Spin the spinner to decide who starts the game. Whoever has the greater number goes first.

   Player 1: Spin the spinner. Figure out what number is represented on the Ten-Frame Spinner. Then figure out what number you need to make 10. For example, suppose you spin 7. What number do you need to make 10? (3)

   If the 3 Number Card is turned over, pick it up and write two number sentences: $7 + 3 = 10$ and $10 - 7 = 3$. If it is not, turn over one more card from the deck. If you draw a 3, write the two number sentences.

   Now, it is Player 2's turn to spin. Player 2: If you can find the missing addend among the Number Cards already turned over, pick up the card. If not, turn over one more card from the deck. If you turn over the card you need to make 10, write your two number sentences.

   Keep taking turns until all the cards in the deck have been turned over.

   When the last card is turned over, each player gets one more spin.

   The winner is the player with more cards.

4. Allow time for students to complete the task.

# ⊘ Assessing Student Responses

The following questions will help you assess your students' responses to the activity:

- Did the student(s) determine the correct missing addend?

- Did the student(s) write the correct addition and subtraction number sentences for each toss?

- Did the student(s) use any noticeable fact strategies in finding the differences?

- If a student gave incorrect answers to several problems after determining the number represented on the ten-frame correctly, was any pattern evident?

# 42: Teens

## ⓘ Number of Students

Pairs

## ⊘ Materials

For each student:

- 10 Unifix Cubes for each student

For each pair of students:

- 2 sets of Number Cards 3–18 (pages 117–118)
- Ten-Frame Spinner (page 162)

## ◈ Overview

In this activity students find a missing addend to make a group between 13 and 19.

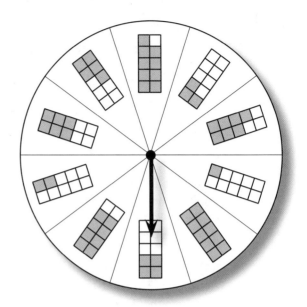

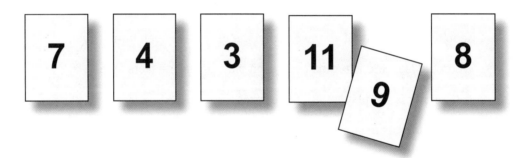

# Presenting the Activity

1. Distribute the Number Cards and spinner to each pair. Below is a list of Number Cards to use for each game:

   - Thirsty Thirteen     3–12
   - Frisky Fourteen     4–13
   - Fancy Fifteen     5–14
   - Sweet Sixteen     6–15
   - Swift Seventeen     7–16
   - Eager Eighteen     8–17
   - Nifty Nineteen     9–18

2. Distribute 10 Unifix Cubes to each student.

3. Say to the students:

   " Shuffle the Number Cards and place them facedown between you.

   Each player spins the spinner. Whoever has the greater number goes first.

   Say to the students:

   Now, turn over six cards and place them in a row.

   For this game, you are going to play "Name-teen."

   Player 1 spins the spinner. Figure out what number is represented on the ten-frames. For example, suppose you spin 7. What number do you need to make 13? (6)

   For example, if the 6 Number Card is turned over, pick it up and write two number sentences: 7 + 6 = 13 and 13 − 7 = 6. If it is not, turn over one more card from the deck.

   Now, it is Player 2's turn to spin. If Player 2 can find the missing addend among the Number Cards already turned over, he or she picks up the card. If not, Player 2 turns over one more card from the deck.

   Keep taking turns until all the cards in the deck have been turned over.

When the last card is turned over, each player gets one more spin.

The winner is the player with more cards.

4. Allow time for students to complete the task.

5. When all pairs have completed a game, have students repeat the game with a different teen number from 13 to 19.

# Assessing Student Responses

The following questions will help you assess your students' responses to the activity:

- Did the student(s) determine the correct missing addend?

- Did the student (s) write the correct addition and subtraction number sentences for each toss?

- Did the student (s) use any noticeable fact strategies in finding the differences?

- If the student(s) answered several problems incorrectly after determining the number represented on the ten-frame correctly, was any pattern evident?

# 43: Build It, Show It

## ⓘ Number of Students

Entire class in partner pairs

## ⊘ Materials

For each pair of students:

- 60 Unifix Cubes
- 6 ten-frames or 3 copies of Ten-Frames Template (page 110)
- "Build It, Show It" Tens Cards (pages 163) 10, 20, 30, 40, 50 in 2 sections of the cards—for example:

- "Build It, Show It" Ones Cards 0–9 (page 163)
- "Build It, Show It" Number Cards with numbers 48, 17, 33, 52, 28, and 30 (page 164)

## ⟐ Overview

In this activity, students model a two-digit number by using ten-frames, Unifix Cubes, and Place Value Cards to represent the tens and ones.

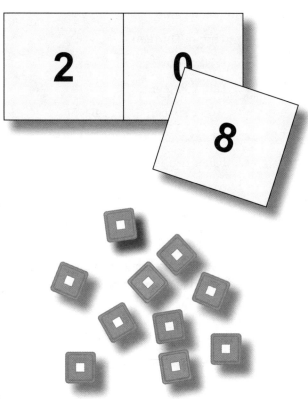

## Common Core State Standards

### Content Standards:

**Grade Level:** 1

**Domain:** Operations and Algebraic Thinking (1.OA)

**Add and subtract within 20.**

6. Understand that the two digits of a two-digit number represent amounts of tens and ones. Understand the following as special cases:

   a. 10 can be thought of as a bundle of ten ones—called a "ten."

   b. The numbers from 11 to 19 are composed of a ten and one, two, three, four, five, six, seven, eight, or nine ones.

   c. The numbers 10, 20, 30, 40, 50, 60, 70, 80, 90 refer to one, two, three, four, five, six, seven, eight, or nine tens (and 0 ones).

### Practice Standards:

2. **Reason abstractly and quantitatively.**

   Students must make sense of the quantity involved in each number called.

4. **Model with mathematics.**

   Students must connect representations and explain the connections.

7. **Look for and make use of structure.**

   Students must understand that the number 46 is four tens and six ones. Understanding that the numbers 10, 20, 30, 40 (and so on) mean one ten, two tens, three tens, four tens (and so on) helps students identify the patterns in the number system.

# Presenting the Activity

1. Make copies of the Place Value Cards and cut the cards apart.

2. Keep the cards face up in two piles between players (a pile for "tens" cards and a pile for "ones" cards).

3. Make copies of the "Build It, Show It" Tens and Ones Cards and cut the cards apart. Place the cards facedown in a pile for the teacher to draw.

4. Reproduce and distribute three Ten-Frames Templates per partner pair.

5. Distribute 60 Unifix Cubes to each partner pair.

6. Have the student pairs decide who will be Player 1 and Player 2.

7. Say to the students:

   " I will pick up the top Number Card and call out the number on my card. We will all say the number together out loud.

   Player 1 will model the number called by placing Unifix Cubes on the ten-frames.

   Player 2 will find the Place Value Card that shows the number called.

   For example, suppose the Number Card is 13. Player 1 will show 13 as follows:

   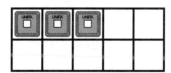

8. Say to the students:

   " Player 2 will find two Place Value Cards from the two piles. One card will be the 10 card and the other will be the 3 card.

Player 2 will place the 3 card on top of the 0 placeholder of the tens card, as shown here, to create the number 13.

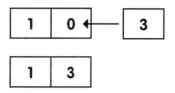

9. Say to the students:

   " Each player will look at his or her partner's work to see whether they have placed the cards correctly.

10. Round two will begin with players switching roles. Player 1 will use the Tens and Ones Cards as Player 2 uses the ten-frames with Unifix Cubes to model the number called.

# Assessing Student Responses

The following questions will help you assess your students' responses to the activity.

- Did the student(s) correctly model the number called?

- Did student(s) understand that the numbers 10, 20, 30, 40, and 50 refer to one, two, three, four, and five tens (and 0 ones)?

- Did the student(s) understand that the number meaning refers to the concept of place value: groups of tens with ones left over?

- Did the student(s) explain their thinking to each other?

# 44: Comparatively Speaking

## ⓘ Number of Students

Partner pairs

## ⊘ Materials

For each pair of students:

- "Comparatively Speaking" Number Card pairs: 21 and 12, 32 and 23, 14 and 43, 33 and 26 (page 165)
- 2 ten-frames or Ten-Frames Template (page 110)
- Unifix Cubes

For each student:

- Individual student whiteboard and marker (or create a recording page)

## ◈ Overview

In this activity, students compare two numbers with Unifix Cubes and ten-frames, first by looking at the number of tens, then, if needed, the number of ones to determine the greater and the lesser number.

43 > 14

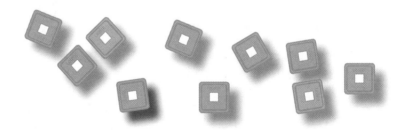

## Common Core State Standards

### Content Standards:

**Grade Level:** 1

**Domain:** Number and Operations in Base Ten (1.NBT)

**Understand place value.**

3. Compare two two-digit numbers based on meanings of the tens and ones digits, recording the results of comparisons with the symbols >, =, and <.

### Practice Standards:

2. **Reason abstractly and quantitatively.**

   Students must make sense of the quantity involved and be able to compare two-digit numbers.

4. **Model with mathematics.**

   Students make sense of place value by modeling and comparing two sets of numbers.

# ⬛ Presenting the Activity

1. Make copies of the set of 4 Number Card pairs and cut the cards apart.

2. Place the 4 cards facedown between both players.

3. Distribute the Ten-Frames Template and 60 Unifix Cubes to each partner pair.

4. Distribute individual student whiteboards and markers to each student.

5. Determine who will be Player 1 and Player 2.

6. Say to the students:

   > 〝 A set of four cards has been placed between you and your partner.
   >
   > Player 1 will turn over the first card so both of you can see the numbers on the card.
   >
   > Player 1 will use Unifix Cubes and ten-frames to show his/her number.
   >
   > Player 2 will use Unifix Cubes to show his or her number.
   >
   > After both of you have modeled your numbers with cubes, compare the two numbers by first looking at the number of tens and then, if needed, looking at the number of ones.
   >
   > Use your student whiteboards and markers to write a comparison statement. Use the greater-than or less-than signs.
   >
   > After you have written your statements, share them with each other to see if you are both correct.

7. The process is repeated for the remaining three cards. Player 2 turns over the second card.

# ⊘ Assessing Student Responses

The following questions will help you assess your students' responses to the activity.

- Did the student(s) correctly model the numbers on the cards using Unifix Cubes and ten-frames?

- Did the student(s) compare the two numbers by first looking at the number of tens, then if needed, the number of ones to determine the greater and the lesser number?

- Did the student(s)) correctly compare their numbers using the greater-than and less-than symbols?

- Did the student(s) use correct terminology including *less than, greater than, most, greatest, least, the same as, equal to,* and *not equal to?*

# 45: You Can't Count on It

## (i) Number of Students

Partner pairs

## (/) Materials

For each pair of students:

- "You Can't Count on It" Game Mat (page 166)
- 2 ten-frames or Ten-Frames Template (page 110)
- 100 Unifix Cubes
- 2 two-color counters to use as game board markers
- Paper clip and pencil to use with spinners

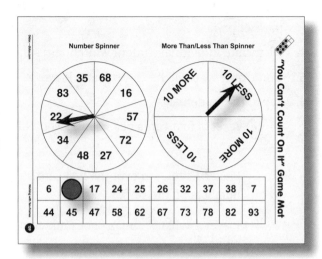

## (◆) Overview

In this activity, partners spin spinners to mentally find 10 more or 10 less than a number.

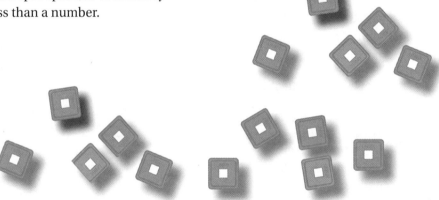

## Common Core State Standards

### Content Standards:

**Grade Level:** 1

**Domain:** Number and Operations in Base Ten (1.NBT)

**Use place value understanding and properties of operations to add and subtract.**

5. Given a two-digit number, mentally find 10 more or 10 less than the number, without having to count; explain the reasoning used.

### Practice Standards:

2. **Reason abstractly and quantitatively.**

   Students must make sense of the quantity involved and be able to compare two-digit numbers.

7. **Look for and make use of structure.**

   Students discover a pattern or structure when adding and subtracting 10.

# ▣ Presenting the Activity

1. Reproduce the "You Can't Count on It" Game Mat.

2. Distribute the two-color counters, Ten-Frames Template, Unifix Cubes, and paper clip and pencil to each partner pair.

3. Say to the students:

   **❝** Partners decide who will start the game.

   Player 1 spins the Number Spinner and then spins the More Than/Less Than Spinner to mentally find 10 more or 10 less than the number.

   For example, suppose Player 1 lands on 25 for the number spin and 10 less than for the second spin. Player 1 must mentally determine the answer without having to count back. Then Player 1 must use the ten-frames to prove his/her answer.

   Player 1 will end his/her play by covering the answer on the game mat with his/her marker.

   Now, Player 2 will spin on the two spinner sheets.

   The player with more markers at the end of five rounds is the winner.

# ◉ Assessing Student Responses

The following questions will help you assess your students' responses to the activity.

- Did the student(s) mentally find 10 more or 10 less without counting?

- Did the student(s) demonstrate how he/she mentally found the answer?

- Did the student(s) see a pattern when adding or subtracting 10, stating something like "10 more than 22 is 32 because 32 is one more ten than 22"?

# 46: Tic-Tac-Toe Subtraction

## ⓘ Number of Students

Entire class

## ⊘ Materials

- Tic-Tac-Toe Game Mat (page 167)
- Tic-Tac-Toe Problem Cards (page 168)
- 10 ten-frames or Ten-Frames Template (page 110)
- 100 Unifix Cubes
- Large whiteboard and marker to draw and display Tic-Tac-Toe Game Mat
- Document camera (if available) to show Problem Cards and model subtraction problems

## ◈ Overview

In this activity, students play Tic-Tac-Toe as a class divided into two teams. The game will allow students to practice subtracting multiples of ten and explain their thinking.

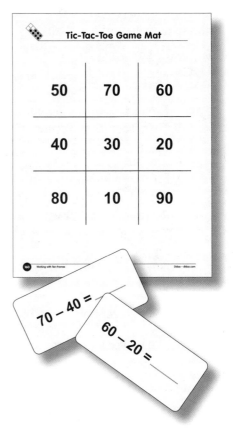

## Common Core State Standards

### Content Standards:

**Grade Level:** 1

**Domain:** Number and Operations in Base Ten (1.NBT)

**Use place value understanding and properties of operations to add and subtract.**

6. Subtract multiples of 10 in the range 10–90 from multiples of 10 in the range 10–90 (positive or zero differences), using concrete models or drawings and strategies based on place value, properties of operations, and/or the relationship between addition and subtraction; relate the strategy to a written method and explain the reasoning used.

### Practice Standards:

2. **Reason abstractly and quantitatively.**

   Students will make sense of the quantity and connect it to a written method, specifically explaining the reasoning used.

3. **Construct viable arguments and critique the reasoning of others.**

   Students will construct arguments using ten-frames and explain their thinking. Students will also listen to other students and communicate whether the explanations make sense.

4. **Model with mathematics.**

   Students will represent subtraction with ten-frames to demonstrate their thinking.

7. **Look for and make use of structure.**

   Studentx will discover a pattern or structure.

# ⬛ Presenting the Activity

1. Make a copy of the Tic-Tac-Toe Mat.

2. Make a copy of the Tic-Tac-Toe Problem Cards and cut them apart. Shuffle the cards and place them facedown.

3. Make 10 copies of the Ten-Frames Template.

4. Gather 100 Unifix Cubes.

5. Prepare document camera to show the Tic-Tac-Toe problems.

6. Draw the Tic-Tac-Toe Game Mat on the white board for the class to view.

7. Divide the class into two teams.

8. Say to the students:

   > A member of Team 1 will begin by selecting the top Tic-Tac-Toe Problem Card and place it on the document camera for other students to view.
   >
   > I will read the selected card out loud.
   >
   > All students will then turn to a partner to discuss how to solve the problem.
   >
   > After a few minutes, a Team 1 player will share the answer to the Problem Card. The player's team can help, if necessary.
   >
   > The Team 1 player must subtract multiples of 10 using the ten-frames or strategies based on place value. The player must explain the thinking involved in solving the problem and connect it to the written method.
   >
   > If the Team 1 player is correct, an X may be marked on the Tic-Tac-Toe board in the location of the answer.
   >
   > Team 2 will select a problem to solve and do the same thing.
   >
   > Three X's or O's in a row wins.

# ⬛ Assessing Student Responses

The following questions will help you assess your students' responses to the activity.

- Did the student(s) use the ten-frames and Unifix Cubes to demonstrate and justify their thinking?

- Did the student(s) correctly subtract?

- Did the student(s) explain their subtraction strategy based on place value? For example, in the problem 60 – 30, did the student say something like "6 tens subtract 3 tens is 3 tens, or 50 (one ten), 40 (two tens), 30 (three tens)"?

# 47: I Have, Who Has?

## ⓘ Number of Students

Small group or entire class

## ⊘ Materials

For the group:
- "I Have, Who Has?" Cards (pages 169–172)

## ◈ Overview

In this activity students read aloud a brief description about a number (beginning with the phrase "I have . . ."). The student who has that number then reads aloud a statement about a new number, beginning with the phrase "Who has . . . ?" The process continues until it cycles back to the first student.

I have 3. Who has double 3?

## Common Core State Standards

### Content Standards:

**Grade Level:** 1

**Domain:** Operations and Algebraic Thinking (1.OA)

**Add and subtract within 20.**

6. Add and subtract within 20, demonstrating fluency for addition and subtraction within 10.

**Domain:** Number and Operations in Base Ten (1.NBT)

**Use place value understanding and properties of operations to add and subtract.**

5. Given a two-digit number, mentally find 10 more or 10 less than the number, without having to count; explain the reasoning used.

### Practice Standards:

2. **Reason abstractly and quantitatively.**

   Students have been making 10 using various strategies, such as counting on. They have also been counting back. Similar strategies work for finding sums or differences to 20.

6. **Attend to precision.**

   Students recognize representations of numbers, and communicate further information about a new number.

# ⊡ Presenting the Activity

1.  The activity uses all 20 "I Have, Who Has?" Cards. Make a copy of the cards and distribute at least one card to each student.

2.  Say to the student(s):

    **"** To start the activity, I will have one of you read the left side of your card. Whoever has ten-frames showing that number then reads his or her card.

    We will eventually end up with whoever started.

3.  You may need to demonstrate the activity with two cards.

4.  Allow time for students to complete the activity.

# ⊙ Assessing Student Responses

The following questions will help you assess your students' responses to the activities:

*   Did the student(s) correctly identify that their card showed the number being described? If not, what errors were made?

*   How did the student(s) determine the correct answers?

# 48: All Aboard My Unifix Train

## ⓘ Number of Students

Partner pairs

## ⊘ Materials

For each student:

- "All Aboard My Unifix Train" Mat (page 174)

For each pair of students:

- "All Aboard My Unifix Train" Cards (page 173)
- 20 Unifix ten-frame trains (commercially available)
- 100 Unifix Cubes

## ◈ Overview

In this activity, students use Unifix Cubes to create groups of ten by adding and subtracting.

## Common Core State Standards

### Content Standards:

**Grade Level:** 1

**Domain:** Number and Operations in Base Ten (1.NBT)

**Use place value understanding and properties of operations to add and subtract.**

4. Add within 100, including adding a two-digit number and a one-digit number, and adding a two-digit number and a multiple of 10, using concrete models or drawings and strategies based on place value, properties of operations, and/or the relationship between addition and subtraction; relate the strategy to a written method and explain the reasoning used. Understand that in adding two-digit numbers, one adds tens and tens, ones and ones; and sometimes it is necessary to compose a ten.

### Practice Standards:

2. **Reason abstractly and quantitatively.**

   Students will make sense of quantity.

4. **Model with mathematics.**

   Students will add and subtract with ten-frames.

7. **Look for and make use of structure.**

   Students will discover a pattern or structure.

## 🔲 Presenting the Activity

1. Make copies of the "All Aboard My Unifix Train" Cards and Mat.

2. Group the students into partner pairs.

3. Distribute 20 Unifix ten-frame trains and 100 Unifix Cubes to each partner pair

4. Give each student an "All Aboard My Unifix Train" Mat.

5. Say to the students:

   > 66 Place 10 Unifix Cubes on the Unifix Cube ten-frame train or make a train by joining 10 Unifix Cubes.
   >
   > Place the 10-cube train you just made on your mat. We'll call your mat the train station.
   >
   > With your partner, decide who will play first.
   >
   > Player 1 will shuffle the "All Aboard My Unifix Train" Cards and place them facedown between both players.
   >
   > Player 1 will draw the top card and follow the directions on the card.
   >
   > For example, if the card reads: + 8 cubes, Player 1 will begin creating a new train by joining 8 cubes.
   >
   > Your goal is to make a 10-cube train. Every time you complete a 10-cube train, you may take the train to the train station.
   >
   > If you need to subtract cubes from your train but you do not have enough, you can take one of your trains from the station and take off the cubes you need.
   >
   > If you need to subtract cubes from your train but you do not have enough and do not have a 10-cube train at the station, you lose your turn.
   >
   > You will play 6 rounds.
   >
   > At the end of the 6 rounds, the player with more 10-cube trains at the station is the winner.

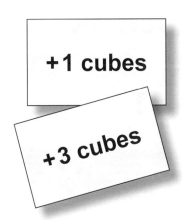

## ✓ Assessing Student Responses

The following questions will help you assess the student responses to the activity.

• Did the student(s) use the Unifix Cubes to create groups of tens?

• Did the student(s) correctly add and/or subtract?

• Did the student(s) explain his/her addition or subtraction strategy based on place value?

# 49: Solitaire to 20

## ⓘ Number of Students

Individual or partner pairs

## ✏ Materials

- Ten-Frame Cards 1–20 (pages 114–115)
- "Solitaire to 20" Number Cards 1–20 (pages 175–176)

## ◈ Overview

In this individual game, students combine Ten-Frame Cards and Number Cards to make sums of 20.

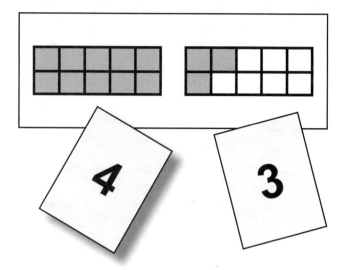

**13 + 4 + 3 = 20**

## Common Core State Standards

### Content Standards:

**Grade Level:** 1

**Domain:** Operations and Algebraic Thinking (1.OA)

**Add and subtract within 20.**

6. Add and subtract within 20, demonstrating fluency for addition and subtraction within 10.

**Domain:** Number and Operations in Base Ten (1.NBT)

**Use place value understanding and properties of operations to add and subtract.**

4. Add within 100, including adding a two-digit number and a one-digit number, and adding a two-digit number and a multiple of 10, using concrete models or drawings and strategies based on place value, properties of operations, and/or the relationship between addition and subtraction; relate the strategy to a written method and explain the reasoning used. Understand that in adding two-digit numbers, one adds tens and tens, ones and ones; and sometimes it is necessary to compose a ten.

### Practice Standards:

1. **Make sense of problems and persevere in solving them.**

   Students must make connections between ten-frames representations of numbers and number symbols that sum to 20.

7. **Look for and express regularity in repeated reasoning.**

   Students observe repeated representations of numbers on ten-frames and the missing addend that makes a sum of 20.

# ⓘ Presenting the Activity

1. Make copies of the Ten-Frame Cards and Number Cards on card stock and cut them apart.

2. Distribute a set of Ten-Frame Cards and a set of Number Cards to each student. The combined deck will contain 40 cards.

3. Say to the student(s):

   " Place the deck of cards in front of you.

   Turn over 6 cards in a row. Now pick up 1, 2, or 3 cards that have a sum of 20.

   After you pick up cards, replace them with cards from the deck so there are always 6 cards showing.

   Each time you pick up cards, write a number sentence showing the addends. If you pick up the "20" card, write $20 = 20$.

   The game is over when you can no longer pick up cards.

   Count the cards that you picked up.

   Then play the game again.

4. You may need to demonstrate the game by showing cards that sum to 20 using 1, 2, or 3 cards.

5. Allow time for students to complete the game.

# ⊘ Assessing Student Responses

The following questions will help you assess your students' responses to the activity:

- Did the student(s) correctly find cards that sum to 20?

- Did the student(s) combine three cards on any particular turn?

- Did the student(s) miss combinations that had a sum of 20?

# 50: The Answer to My Problem Is

## (i) Number of Students

Entire class with partner pairs, or small group

## (/) Materials

For each pair of students:

- 20 Unifix Cubes

For each student:

- 2 ten-frames or Ten-Frames Template (page 110)

For the teacher:

- Individual student whiteboard and marker or document camera and pencil/paper
- Large classroom whiteboard and marker

##  Overview

In this activity, students are given the answer to an addition or subtraction problem and must try to figure out what the problem is.

The answer to my problem is 12.

## Common Core State Standards

### Content Standards:

**Grade Level:** 1

**Domain:** Operations and Algebraic Thinking (1.OA)

**Add and subtract within 20.**

6. Add and subtract within 20, demonstrating fluency for addition and subtraction within 10.

### Practice Standards:

2. **Reason abstractly and quantitatively.**
   Students make sense of quantity.

4. **Model with mathematics.**
   Students add and subtract with ten-frames.

7. **Look for and make use of structure.**
   Students discover a pattern or structure.

# ⬛ Presenting the Activity

1. Distribute two ten-frames or make a copy of the Ten-Frames Template for each student.

2. Distribute 20 Unifix Cubes per partner pair.

3. Say to the students:

   > **(66)** I will begin our activity by writing a problem on the individual whiteboard. I will hide the problem so that you cannot see it yet.
   >
   > I will tell you the answer to the problem.
   >
   > For example, I might say, "The answer to my problem is 11. What is my problem?"
   >
   > You may work with your partner. Use the Unifix Cubes and the ten-frames, if necessary, to decide what the problem is.
   >
   > Come up with several different problems that have the answer (11).

4. After a few minutes, say to the students:

   > **(66)** Now that you have had a few minutes to work with your partner, who thinks they know what the problem is?

5. Call on a student. Put the student's response on the large whiteboard. For example, the student might say, "Is your problem $5 + 6 = 11$?"

6. If the student has guessed the problem correctly, say:

   > **(66)** Yes, my problem is $5 + 6 = 11$.

7. Hold up the small whiteboard or use a document camera to show the problem.

8. The student who guessed the answer will create the next problem.

9. If $5 + 6 = 11$ is not the correct problem, say to the students:

   > **(66)** That could be my problem, but that is not what I was thinking.
   >
   > Let's try again with another student.

10. Allow the students five attempts to discover the correct problem. Record each attempt on the large whiteboard for all students to view.

# ✓ Assessing Student Responses

The following questions will help you assess your students' responses to the activity.

- Did the student(s) use the Unifix Cubes to model the addition or subtraction number sentence?

- Did the student(s) correctly add and/or subtract?

- Did the student(s) explain their addition or subtraction strategy?

# Blackline Masters
## Table of Contents

# Ten-Frames Template

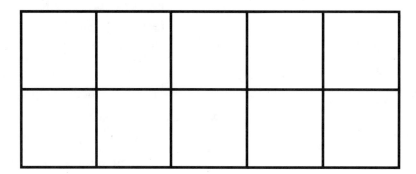

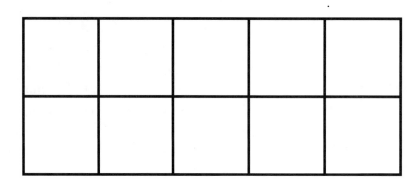

# Object Cards 1–8

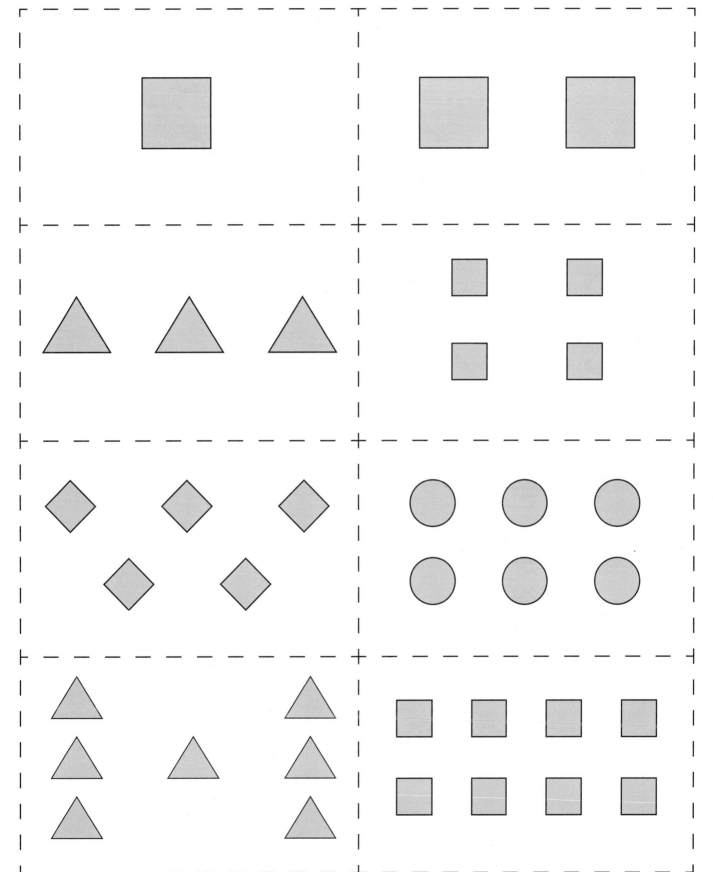

# Object Cards 9–16

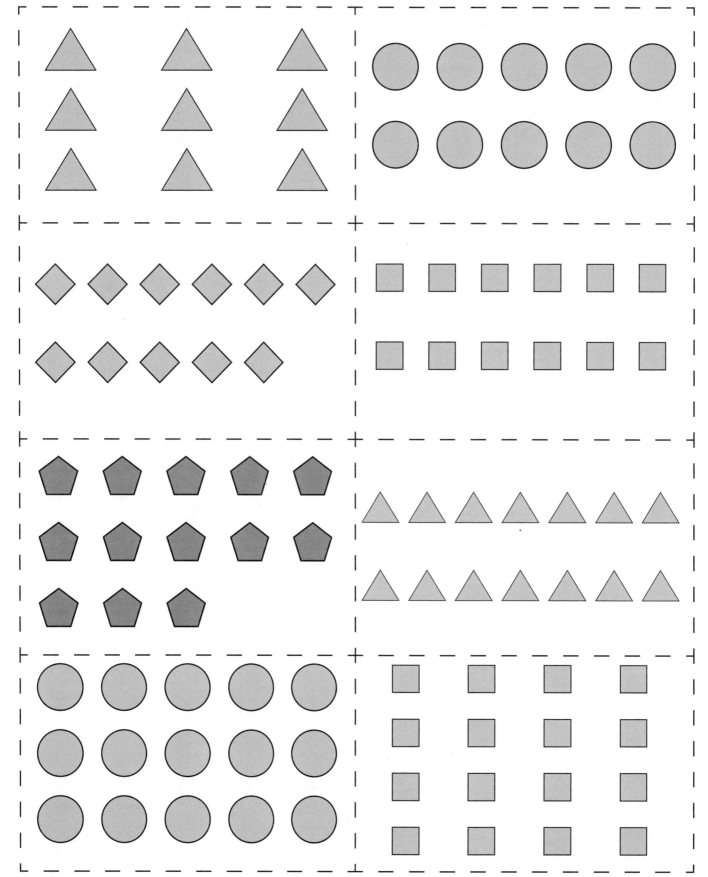

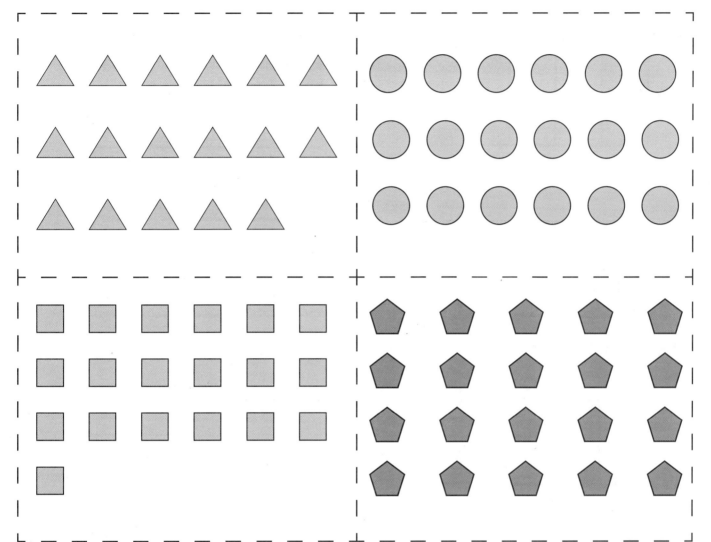

# Ten-Frame Cards 1–10

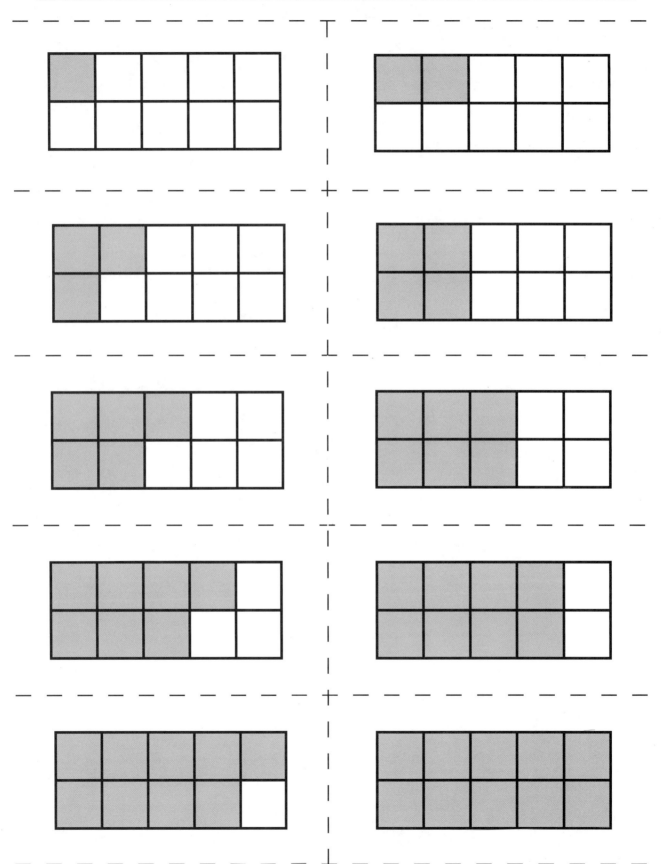

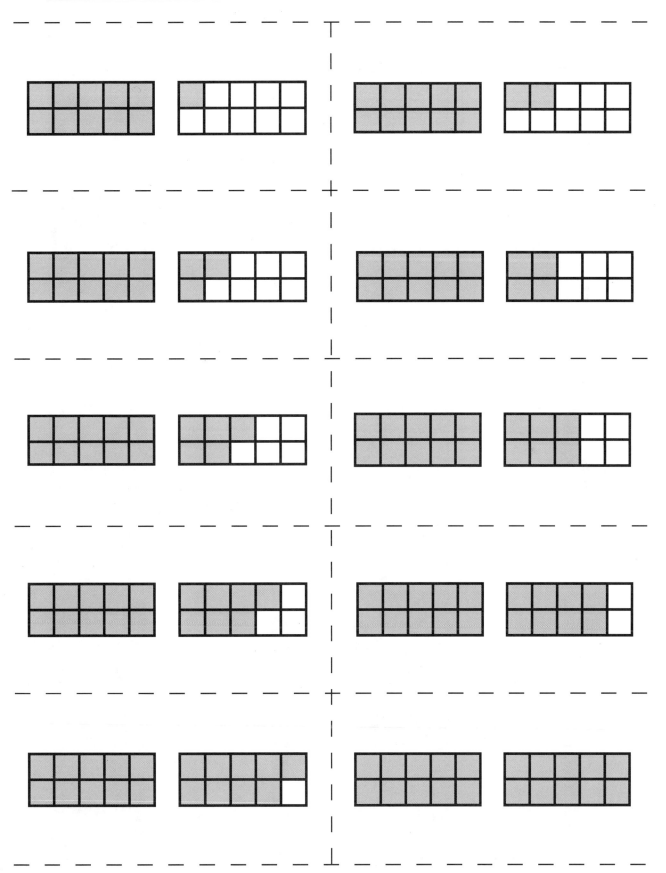

# Cell-Phone Picture Cards

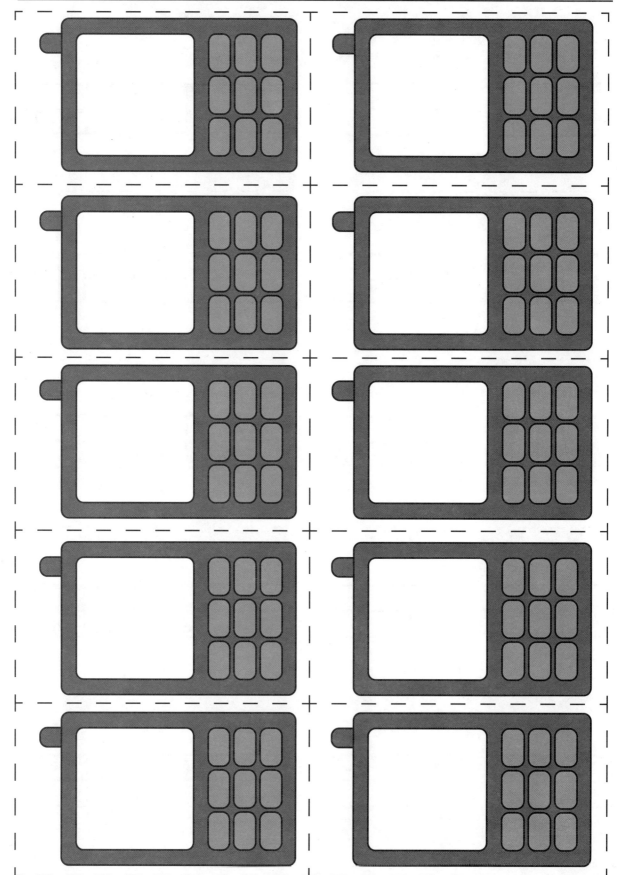

# Number Cards 1–9

1    2    3

4    5    6

7    8    9

10 | 11 | 12

13 | 14 | 15

16 | 17 | 18

19 | 20 | 21

22 | 23 | 24

25 | 26 | 27

**28** **29** **30**

**0**

# Number Word Cards

| | |
|---|---|
| **one** | **two** |
| **three** | **four** |
| **five** | **six** |
| **seven** | **eight** |
| **nine** | **ten** |

# Number Word Cards

eleven

twelve

thirteen

fourteen

fifteen

sixteen

seventeen

eighteen

nineteen

twenty

# "One More Than" Recording Sheet

_____ + 1 = _____          _____ + 1 = _____

_____ + 1 = _____          _____ + 1 = _____

_____ + 1 = _____          _____ + 1 = _____

_____ + 1 = _____          _____ + 1 = _____

_____ + 1 = _____          _____ + 1 = _____

_____ + 1 = _____          _____ + 1 = _____

**"One Less Than" Recording Sheet**

_____ – 1 = _____          _____ – 1 = _____

_____ – 1 = _____          _____ – 1 = _____

_____ – 1 = _____          _____ – 1 = _____

_____ – 1 = _____          _____ – 1 = _____

_____ – 1 = _____          _____ – 1 = _____

_____ – 1 = _____          _____ – 1 = _____

# "Flashing Numbers" Activity Sheet 1

A. _____

B. _____

C. _____

D. _____

E. _____

F. _____

G. _____

H. _____

I. _____

J. _____

K. _____

# "Flashing Numbers" Activity Sheet 2

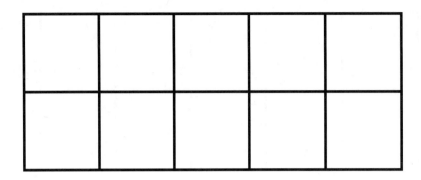

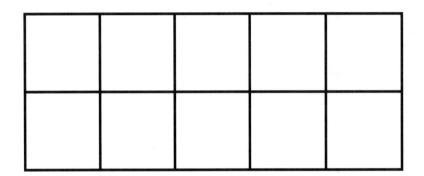

A. _____

B. _____

C. _____

D. _____

E. _____

F. _____

G. _____

H. _____

I. _____

J. _____

K. _____

# Take-Away Cards

| Take away 1 | Take away 2 |
| --- | --- |
| Take away 3 | Take away 4 |
| Take away 5 | Take away 6 |
| Take away 7 | Take away 8 |
| Take away 9 | Take away 10 |

# "Take Away" Activity Sheet 1

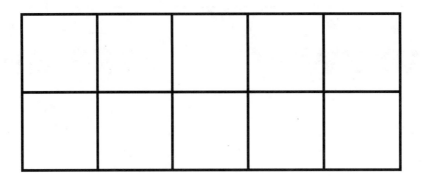

10 – _____ = _____          10 – _____ = _____

10 – _____ = _____          10 – _____ = _____

10 – _____ = _____          10 – _____ = _____

10 – _____ = _____          10 – _____ = _____

10 – _____ = _____          10 – _____ = _____

# "Take Away" Activity Sheet 2

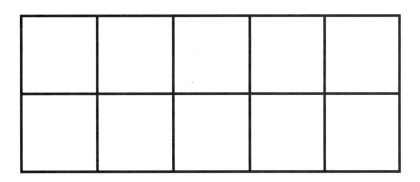

_____ − _____ = _____          _____ − _____ = _____

_____ − _____ = _____          _____ − _____ = _____

_____ − _____ = _____          _____ − _____ = _____

_____ − _____ = _____          _____ − _____ = _____

_____ − _____ = _____          _____ − _____ = _____

# "My Missing Number of Cubes" Recording Sheet

| My number of cubes: _____ | I see _____ cubes. | _____ cubes are hiding. |
|---|---|---|

**Show this with cubes:**

**Another way to make _____ is:**
**(Show this with cubes.)**

# "Another Way" Activity Sheet

## Sum = _____

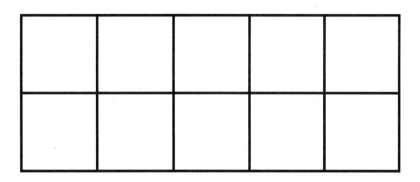

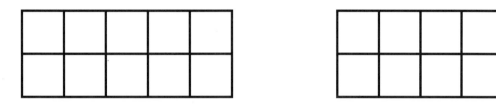

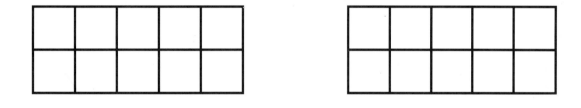

# "Make Ten" Activity Sheet

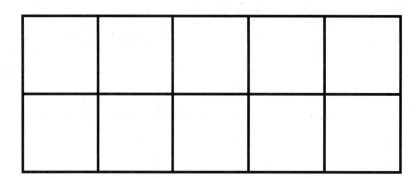

_____ + _____ = 10    _____ + _____ = 10

_____ + _____ = 10    _____ + _____ = 10

_____ + _____ = 10    _____ + _____ = 10

_____ + _____ = 10    _____ + _____ = 10

_____ + _____ = 10    _____ + _____ = 10

_____ + _____ = 10

# "Spin to Win" Spinner

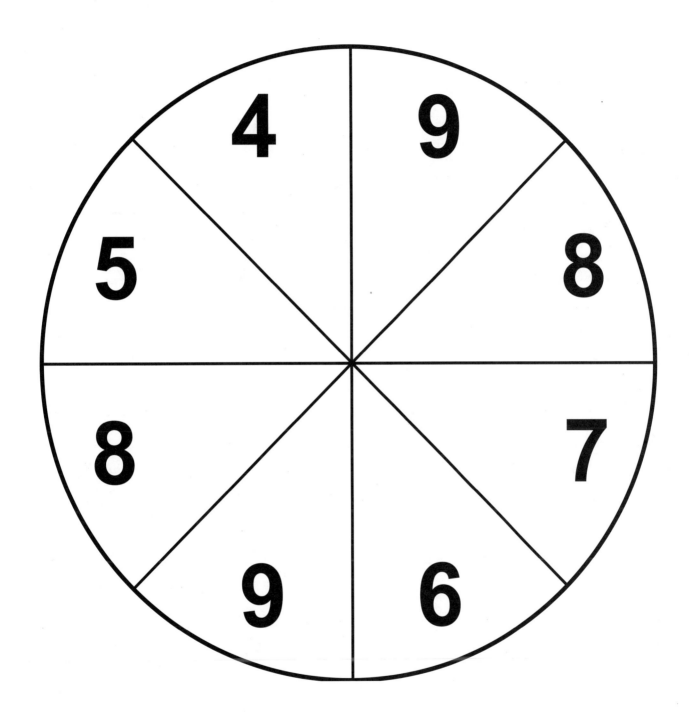

# "Spin to Win" Recording Sheet

|  | Player 1 | Player 2 |
|---|---|---|
| **Round 1** | 1 group of ten and _____ = _____ | 1 group of ten and _____ = _____ |
| **Round 2** | 1 group of ten and _____ = _____ | 1 group of ten and _____ = _____ |
| **Round 3** | 1 group of ten and _____ = _____ | 1 group of ten and _____ = _____ |
| **Round 4** | 1 group of ten and _____ = _____ | 1 group of ten and _____ = _____ |
| **Round 5** | 1 group of ten and _____ = _____ | 1 group of ten and _____ = _____ |

one ten and 1 one

one ten and 2 ones

one ten and 3 ones

one ten and 4 ones

one ten and 5 ones

one ten and 6 ones

one ten and 7 ones

one ten and 8 ones

one ten and 9 ones

# 11–19 Spinner

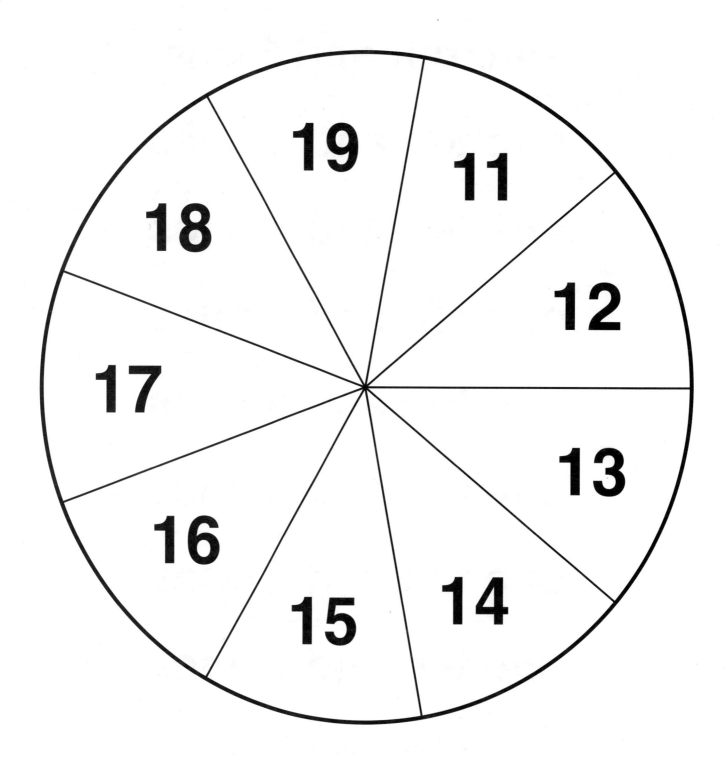

# Place Value Game Board 1

| | | |
|---|---|---|
| One ten and 4 ones | One ten and 2 ones | One ten and 1 one | Two tens and 0 ones |
| One ten and 3 ones | One ten and 5 ones | Free Space | One ten and 0 ones |
| One ten and 7 ones | One ten and 6 ones | One ten and 8 ones | One ten and 9 ones |

# Place Value Game Board 2

| | | |
|---|---|---|
| Two tens and 0 ones | One ten and 3 ones | One ten and 1 one | One ten and 9 ones |
| One ten and 4 ones | One ten and 5 ones | Free Space | One ten and 2 ones |
| One ten and 0 ones | One ten and 7 ones | One ten and 6 ones | One ten and 8 ones |

# Place Value Game Board 3

| One tens and 0 ones | One ten and 5 ones | One ten and 2 ones | One ten and 6 ones |
|---|---|---|---|
| One ten and 4 ones | One ten and 3 ones | One ten and 1 one | Free Space |
| One ten and 7 ones | One ten and 8 ones | One ten and 9 ones | Two ten and 0 ones |

# Place Value Game Board 4

| | | |
|---|---|---|
| One tens and 2 ones | Free Space | One ten and 7 ones |
| One ten and 3 ones | One ten and 4 ones | One ten and 6 ones |
| One ten and 9 ones | One ten and 0 ones | Two tens and 0 ones |
| One ten and 1 one | One ten and 5 ones | One ten and 8 ones |

# Place Value Caller's Cards

**Place a chip on 10**

**Place a chip on 11**

**Place a chip on 12**

**Place a chip on 13**

**Place a chip on 14**

**Place a chip on 15**

**Place a chip on 16**

**Place a chip on 17**

**Place a chip on 18**

**Place a chip on 19**

**Place a chip on 20**

# "More Than Ten" Activity Sheet

<table>
<tr><td></td><td></td></tr>
<tr><td></td><td></td></tr>
<tr><td></td><td></td></tr>
<tr><td></td><td></td></tr>
<tr><td></td><td></td></tr>
</table>

||     ||     ||     ||     ||

+     +     +     +     +

<table>
<tr><td></td><td></td></tr>
<tr><td></td><td></td></tr>
<tr><td></td><td></td></tr>
<tr><td></td><td></td></tr>
<tr><td></td><td></td></tr>
</table>

||     ||     ||     ||     ||

+     +     +     +     +

# Problem-Solving Cards

I have 6 blue Unifix Cubes and 3 white Unifix Cubes.

How many cubes do I have in all?

---

I have 8 Unifix Cubes in all. There are more blue cubes than white cubes.

How many of each color do I have?

---

I have 7 Unifix Cubes in all. 3 of them are blue.

How many of them are white?

---

I have 5 Unifix Cubes in all. There are more white cubes than blue cubes.

How many of each color do I have?

---

I have 8 Unifix Cubes in all. There are 4 fewer blue cubes than white cubes.

How many of each color do I have?

---

I have 10 Unifix Cubes in all. There are 3 fewer white cubes than blue cubes.

How many of each color do I have?

---

I have more than 6 and fewer than 10 Unifix Cubes in all. 2 of the cubes are blue.

How many of the cubes are white?

---

I have 6 Unifix Cubes in all. There are fewer white cubes than blue cubes.

How many of each color do I have?

# Problem-Solving Cards (Blank)

I have _____ blue Unifix Cubes and _____ white Unifix Cubes.

How many cubes do I have in all?

I have _____ Unifix Cubes in all. There are more blue cubes than white cubes.

How many of each color do I have?

I have _____ Unifix Cubes in all. _____ of them are blue.

How many of them are white?

I have _____ Unifix Cubes in all. There are more white cubes than blue cubes.

How many of each color do I have?

I have _____ Unifix Cubes in all. There are _____ fewer blue cubes than white cubes.

How many of each color do I have?

I have _____ Unifix Cubes in all. There are _____ fewer white cubes than blue cubes.

How many of each color do I have?

I have more than _____ and fewer than _____ Unifix Cubes in all. _____ of the cubes are blue.

How many of the cubes are white?

I have _____ Unifix Cubes in all. There are fewer white cubes than blue cubes.

How many of each color do I have?

# "Who Am I?" Cards

I am between 4 and 8.

I am even.

Who am I?

---

I am less than 16.

I am greater than 12.

I am odd.

Who am I?

---

I am between 14 and 20.

I am odd.

Who am I?

---

I am between 2 and 9.

I am even.

Who am I?

---

I am greater than 10.

I am less than 13.

I am odd.

Who am I?

---

I am less than 10.

I am the number of days
in a week.

Who am I?

---

I am less than 5.

I am greater than 2.

I am even.

Who am I?

---

I am greater than 9.

I am less than 15.

I am even.

I am not 10.

Who am I?

# "Who Am I?" Cards

I am greater than 7 and less than 13.

I am odd.

Who am I?

---

I am less than 9.

I am greater than 3.

I am odd.

Who am I?

---

I am less than 8 and greater than 1.

If I am doubled, I am less than 5.

Who am I?

---

I am even and less than 12.

When I am doubled, I have 0 in the ones place.

Who am I?

---

I am greater than 12.

I am less than 20.

I am even.

Who am I?

---

I am between 13 and 16.

Who am I?

---

I am between 7 and 10.

I am even.

Who am I?

---

I am a 2-digit number. Both of my digits are the same.

Who am I?

# "Who Am I?" Cards

I am a 2-digit number.
My ones digit is 6 more
than my tens digit.

Who am I?

---

I am even.
My double is greater than
13 and less than 18.

Who am I?

---

I am a 2-digit number.
My ones digit is 3 more
than my tens digit.

Who am I?

---

I am odd and less than 12.
When I am doubled, I have
an 8 in the ones place.

Who am I?

---

I am a 2-digit number.
My ones digit is double my
tens digit.

Who am I?

---

I am between 10 and 15.
I am even.

Who am I?

---

I am odd.
My double is greater than
13 and less than 16.

Who am I?

---

I am a 2-digit number.
My ones digit is 8 more
than my tens digit.

Who am I?

# Word Problem Cards

Matt had 14 marbles. Kent gave him 4 more marbles. How many marbles does he have now?

Maggie has 7 stickers. Her sister Mandy has 3 stickers. How many more stickers does Mandy need to have the same number as Maggie?

I want to save 10 pennies. I have 6. How many more pennies do I need to save?

I have 5 teddy bears. My brother has 5 teddy bears. How many bears do we have altogether?

I have 11 shirts. Six of my shirts are blue. How many shirts are not blue?

LaToya collects hair ribbons. She has 4 ribbons now. How many ribbons does she need to collect to have 20 hair ribbons?

Emily read 5 books. To win a prize, she must read 12 books. How many books does she still need to read?

Tim has 19 race cars. He gives 11 to his friend. How many race cars does he have left?

I walked 5 blocks to school, then 6 blocks after school to my friend's house. How many blocks did I walk?

Kevin has 8 pets. Six of his pets are fish in his fish tank. How many pets are dogs?

# "Train Trip" Word Problem Cards

The train traveled 13 miles before the first stop, 4 more miles before the second stop, then 3 more miles and stopped at Union Station. How many miles did the train travel?

---

I love to eat carrots on my trip. I ate 5 carrots for my morning snack, 3 carrots at lunch, and 2 more carrots for dinner.

How many carrots did I eat on my trip?

---

For my long train trip, I took 3 balls, 1 stuffed animal, and 2 board games to play.

How many toys did I take with me?

---

Sitting near me on my trip, I saw 7 boys, 5 girls, and 4 mothers.

How many people did I see?

---

Looking out the train window, I saw 6 robins, 2 bluebirds, and 1 crow.

How many birds did I see in all?

---

Before boarding the train, I saw 5 red railroad cars, 11 blue railroad cars, and 4 yellow railroad cars.

How many railroad cars did I see altogether?

---

Looking out the train window, I saw 15 white buildings, 2 brown buildings, and 1 black building.

How many buildings did I see altogether?

---

On my trip I sang 4 songs, my brother sang 4 songs, and my sister sang 3 songs.

How many songs did we sing in all?

---

The conductor told us we would arrive in 4 minutes. He said it would take us 8 minutes to unload and 5 minutes to get our suitcases. How many minutes in all?

---

On my trip, I wrote 7 notes to my friends, 1 note to my teacher, and 1 note to my grandmother.

How many notes did I write in all?

# Addition Fact Cards

| | | | |
|---|---|---|---|
| 1 + 1 | 1 + 2 | 1 + 3 | 1 + 4 |
| 1 + 5 | 1 + 6 | 1 + 7 | 1 + 8 |
| 1 + 9 | 1 + 10 | 2 + 2 | 2 + 3 |
| 2 + 4 | 2 + 5 | 2 + 6 | 2 + 7 |
| 2 + 8 | 2 + 9 | 2 + 10 | 3 + 3 |

# Addition Fact Cards

| | | | |
|---|---|---|---|
| 3 + 4 | 3 + 5 | 3 + 6 | 3 + 7 |
| 3 + 8 | 3 + 9 | 3 + 10 | 4 + 4 |
| 4 + 5 | 4 + 6 | 4 + 7 | 4 + 8 |
| 4 + 9 | 4 + 10 | 5 + 5 | 5 + 6 |
| 5 + 7 | 5 + 8 | 5 + 9 | 5 + 10 |

# Addition Fact Cards

| | | | |
|---|---|---|---|
| 6 + 6 | 6 + 7 | 6 + 8 | 6 + 9 |
| 6 + 10 | 7 + 7 | 7 + 8 | 7 + 9 |
| 7 + 10 | 8 + 8 | 8 + 9 | 8 + 10 |
| 9 + 9 | 9 + 10 | 10 + 10 | |

# "Addition Action" Activity Sheet

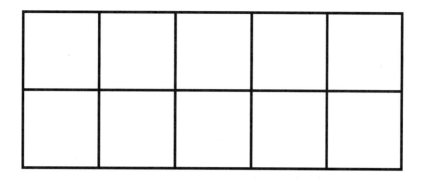

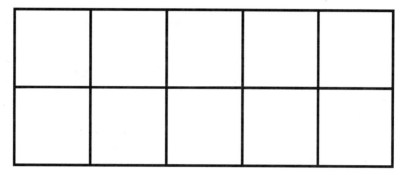

____ + ____ = ____        ____ + ____ = ____

____ + ____ = ____        ____ + ____ = ____

____ + ____ = ____        ____ + ____ = ____

____ + ____ = ____        ____ + ____ = ____

____ + ____ = ____        ____ + ____ = ____

# Subtraction Fact Cards

| | | | |
|---|---|---|---|
| 20 – 15 | 20 – 14 | 20 – 13 | 20 – 12 |
| 20 – 11 | 20 – 10 | 20 – 9 | 20 – 8 |
| 20 – 7 | 20 – 6 | 20 – 5 | 20 – 4 |
| 19 – 13 | 19 – 12 | 19 – 11 | 19 – 10 |
| 19 – 9 | 19 – 8 | 19 – 7 | 19 – 6 |

# Subtraction Fact Cards

| | | | |
|---|---|---|---|
| 19 – 5 | 18 – 12 | 18 – 11 | 18 – 10 |
| 18 – 9 | 18 – 9 | 18 – 7 | 18 – 6 |
| 18 – 5 | 18 – 4 | 17 – 11 | 17 – 10 |
| 17 – 9 | 17 – 8 | 17 – 7 | 17 – 6 |
| 17 – 5 | 16 – 9 | 16 – 8 | 16 – 7 |

# Subtraction Fact Cards

| | | | |
|---|---|---|---|
| 16 – 6 | 16 – 5 | 16 – 4 | 15 – 8 |
| 15 – 7 | 15 – 6 | 15 – 5 | 15 – 4 |
| 15 – 3 | 14 – 7 | 14 – 6 | 14 – 5 |
| 14 – 4 | 13 – 6 | 13 – 5 | 13 – 4 |
| 13 – 3 | | | |

# "Subtraction Action" Activity Sheet

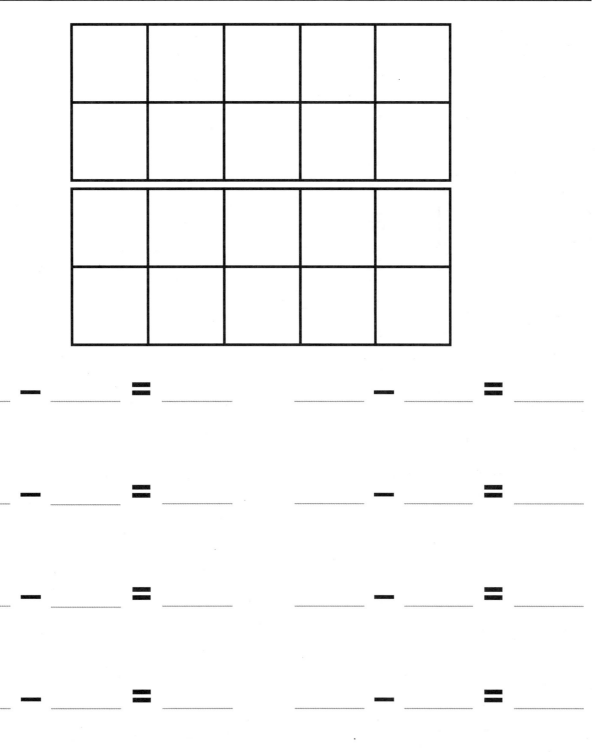

_____ − _____ = _____          _____ − _____ = _____

_____ − _____ = _____          _____ − _____ = _____

_____ − _____ = _____          _____ − _____ = _____

_____ − _____ = _____          _____ − _____ = _____

_____ − _____ = _____          _____ − _____ = _____

# "Make My Target Number" Activity Sheet

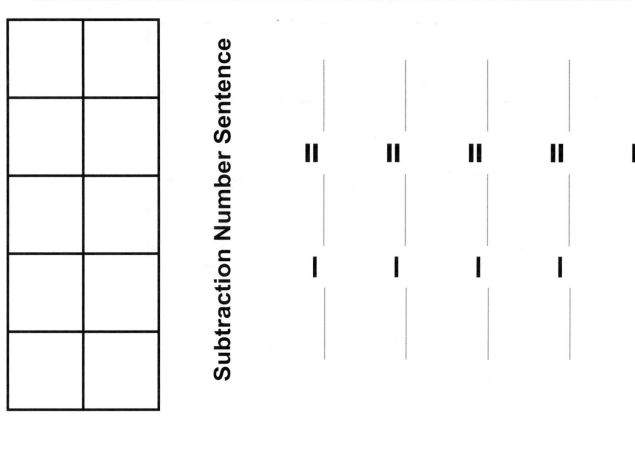

## Subtraction Number Sentence

|       |   |
| ----- | - |
| = | |
| = | |
| = | |
| = | |
| = | |

## Addition Number Sentence

10 + ___ = ___
___ + ___ = ___
___ + ___ = ___
___ + ___ = ___
___ + ___ = ___

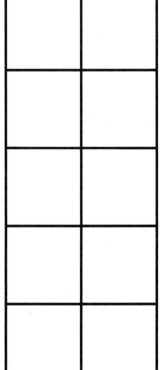

# 1–6 Spinner

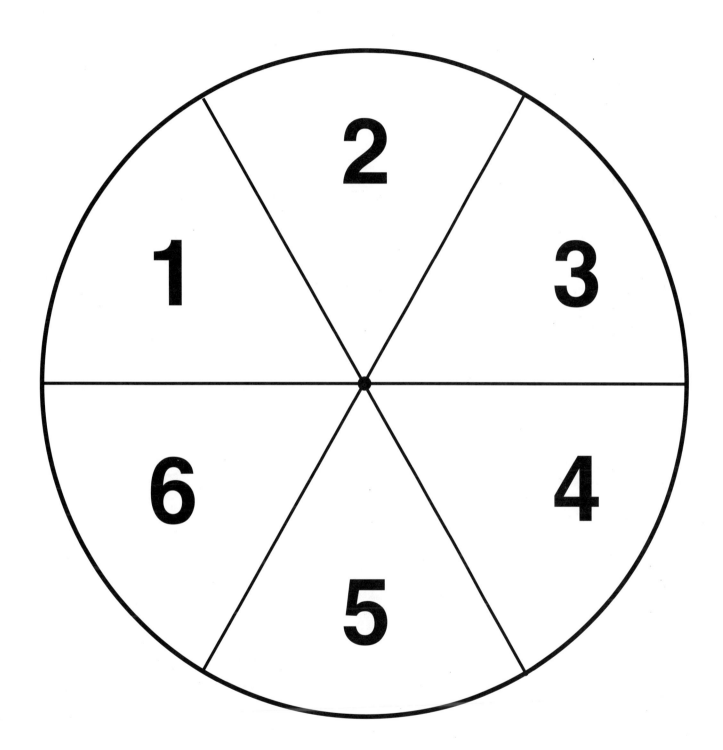

**Working with Ten-Frames**

# "First to 20" Activity Sheet

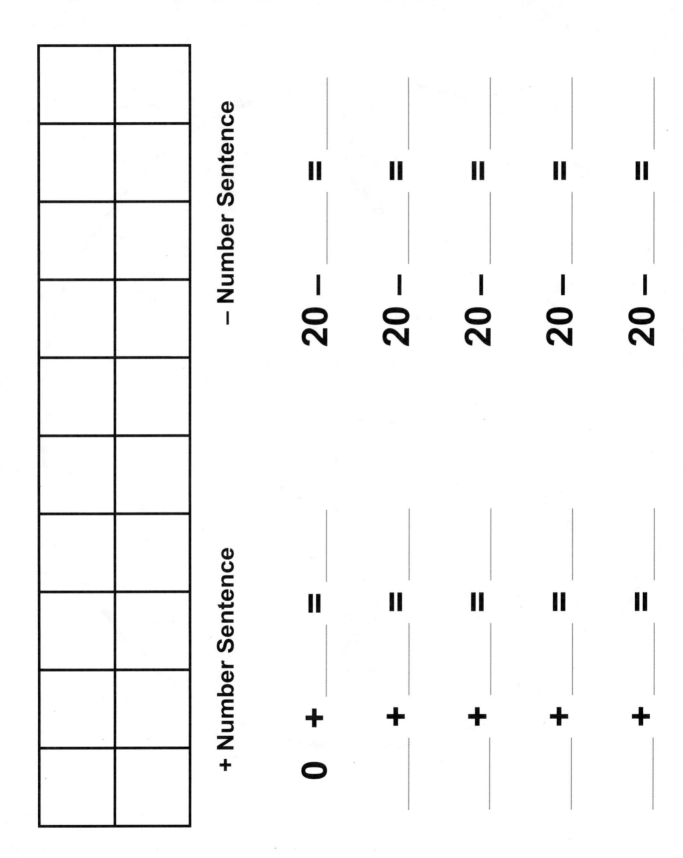

**– Number Sentence**

20 – _____ = _____

20 – _____ = _____

20 – _____ = _____

20 – _____ = _____

20 – _____ = _____

**+ Number Sentence**

0 + _____ = _____

_____ + _____ = _____

_____ + _____ = _____

_____ + _____ = _____

_____ + _____ = _____

# "First to Zero" Activity Sheet

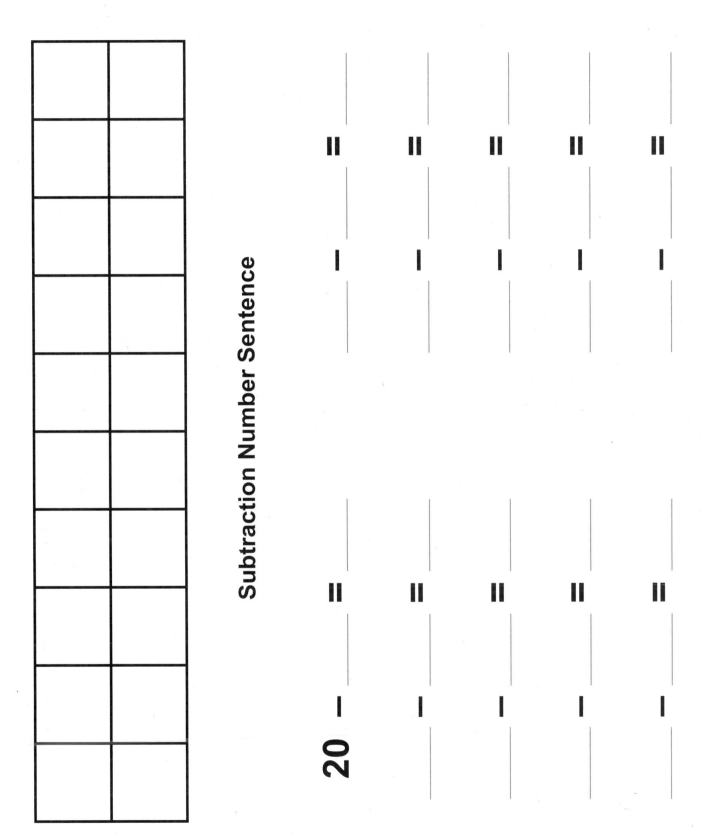

Subtraction Number Sentence

$20$

# Ten-Frame Spinner

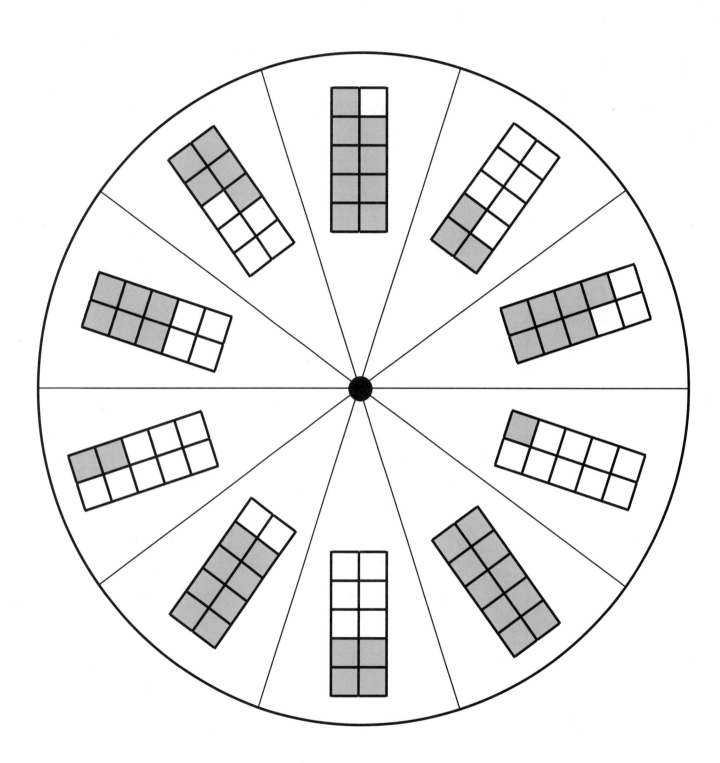

# "Build It, Show It" Tens and Ones Cards

| Tens Cards | | Ones Cards | |
|:---:|:---:|:---:|:---:|
| 1 | 0 | 0 | 1 |
| 2 | 0 | 2 | 3 |
| 3 | 0 | 4 | 5 |
| 4 | 0 | 6 | 7 |
| 5 | 0 | 8 | 9 |

# "Build It, Show It" Number Cards

| | |
|:---:|:---:|
| **48** | **17** |
| **33** | **52** |
| **28** | **30** |

# "Comparatively Speaking" Number Cards

| Player 1 | Player 2 |
|:---:|:---:|
| **21** | **12** |

| Player 1 | Player 2 |
|:---:|:---:|
| **32** | **23** |

| Player 1 | Player 2 |
|:---:|:---:|
| **14** | **43** |

| Player 1 | Player 2 |
|:---:|:---:|
| **33** | **26** |

# "You Can't Count on It" Game Mat

## More Than/Less Than Spinner

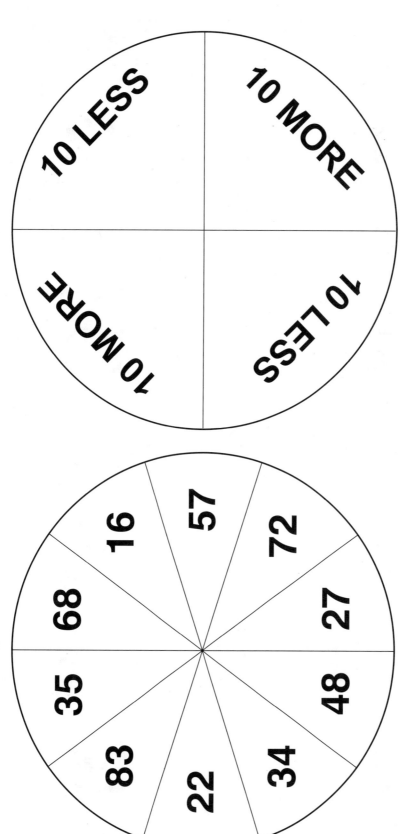

10 LESS

10 MORE

10 MORE

10 LESS

## Number Spinner

16
57
72
27
48
34
22
83
35
68

| | | | | | | |
|---|---|---|---|---|---|---|
| 7 | 38 | 37 | 32 | 26 | 25 | 24 |
| 93 | 82 | 78 | 73 | 67 | 62 | 58 |
| | | | | | | 47 |
| | | | | | | 17 |
| | | | | | | 12 |
| | | | | | | 6 |
| | | | | | | 45 |
| | | | | | | 44 |

|     |     |     |
| --- | --- | --- |
| 50  | 70  | 60  |
| 40  | 30  | 20  |
| 80  | 10  | 90  |

# Tic-Tac-Toe Problem Cards

70 – 40 = _____

60 – 20 = _____

90 – 40 = _____

100 – 40 = _____

100 – 30 = _____

50 – 40 = _____

100 – 20 = _____

80 – 60 = _____

100 – 10 = _____

**Working with Ten-Frames**

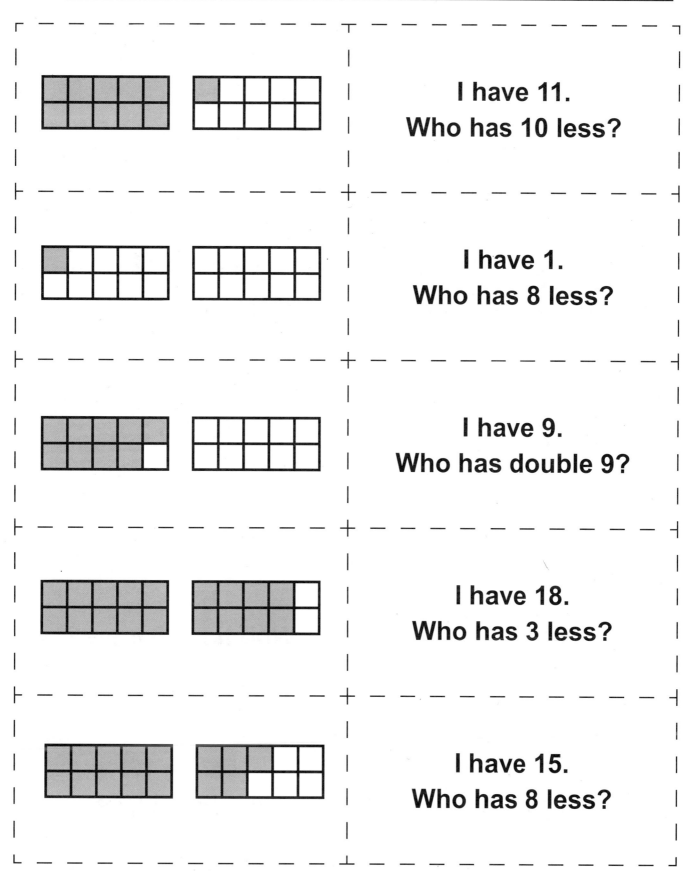

I have 11.
Who has 10 less?

I have 1.
Who has 8 less?

I have 9.
Who has double 9?

I have 18.
Who has 3 less?

I have 15.
Who has 8 less?

# "I Have, Who Has?" Cards

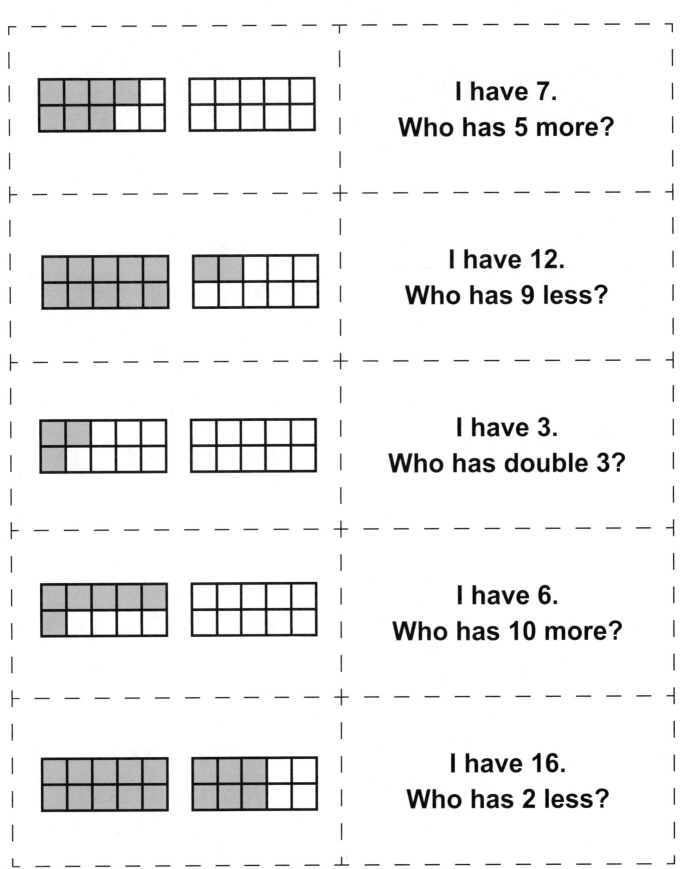

I have 7.
Who has 5 more?

I have 12.
Who has 9 less?

I have 3.
Who has double 3?

I have 6.
Who has 10 more?

I have 16.
Who has 2 less?

# "I Have, Who Has?" Cards

I have 14.
Who has 6 more?

I have 20.
Who has 7 less?

I have 13.
Who has 8 less?

I have 5.
Who has 3 more?

I have 8.
Who has 6 less?

# "I Have, Who Has?" Cards

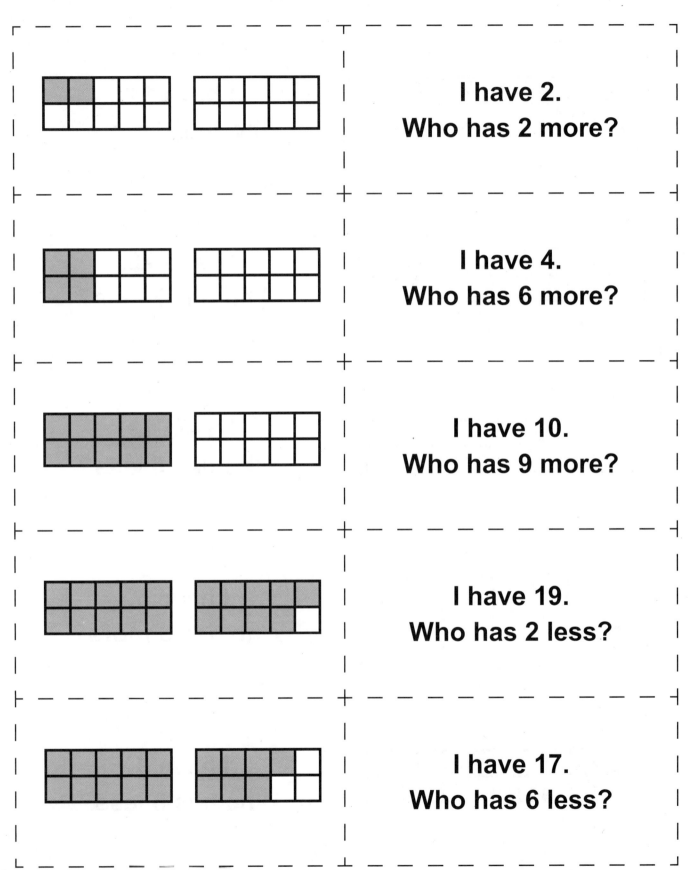

I have 2.
Who has 2 more?

I have 4.
Who has 6 more?

I have 10.
Who has 9 more?

I have 19.
Who has 2 less?

I have 17.
Who has 6 less?

# "All Aboard My Unifix Train" Cards

| | | |
|---|---|---|
| **+1 cubes** | **+2 cubes** | **+3 cubes** |
| **+4 cubes** | **+5 cubes** | **+6 cubes** |
| **+2 cubes** | **+3 cubes** | **+4 cubes** |
| **−1 cubes** | **−2 cubes** | **−3 cubes** |
| **−4 cubes** | **−5 cubes** | **−6 cubes** |
| **−1 cubes** | **−2 cubes** | **−3 cubes** |

# "All Aboard My Unifix Train" Mat

## Player 1 Trains

## Player 2 Trains

1

2

3

4

5

6

7

8

9

10

| | |
|---|---|
| **11** | **12** |
| **13** | **14** |
| **15** | **16** |
| **17** | **18** |
| **19** | **20** |